THE JUDGMENT OF SUSANNA
AUTHORITY AND WITNESS

SOCIETY OF BIBLICAL LITERATURE

EARLY JUDAISM AND ITS LITERATURE

Series Editor
William Adler

Editorial Board

Number 11

THE JUDGMENT OF SUSANNA
AUTHORITY AND WITNESS

edited by
Ellen Spolsky

THE JUDGMENT OF SUSANNA
AUTHORITY AND WITNESS

edited by
Ellen Spolsky

Scholars Press
Atlanta, Georgia

THE JUDGMENT OF SUSANNA
AUTHORITY AND WITNESS

edited by
Ellen Spolsky

Library of Congress Cataloging-in-Publication Data
The Judgment of Susanna : authority and witness / edited by Ellen
Spolsky.
    p. cm. — (Early Judaism and its literature ; no. 11)
Includes bibliographical references.
ISBN 0-7885-0181-X
    1. Bible. O.T. Apocrypha. History of Susanna—Criticism,
interpretation, etc.—History. I. Spolsky, Ellen, 1943–
II. Series.
BS1795.2.J83 1996
229'.6—dc20   96–9567
                        CIP

Printed in the United States of America
on acid-free paper

FOR ELISHEVA
AND ORIAN

Table of Contents

Acknowledgments

Grateful acknowledgment is made to the Lewis Family Fund for International Conferences and The Lechter Institute for Literary Research, sponsors of the symposium at Bar-Ilan University at which earlier versions of the papers collected here were first presented. We are also happy to thank The Italian Cultural Institute and the Israel Association for Canadian Studies for their contributions. Sharon Baris, Aden Bar-Tura, and Betsy Halpern-Amaru all made significant contributions to bringing the symposium and then the collected essays into existence.

INTRODUCTION

The earliest extant version of the Susanna story is in the Old Greek translation of the Hebrew Bible (also referred to as the Septuagint) produced, it is assumed, in 100 B.C.E. In 1947, Carlisle Floyd's opera, *Susanna*, was produced in New York. In between, the story has been told and sung, painted and repainted, in theaters and churches, tombs and palaces. In 1994, the Lechter Institute at Bar-Ilan University convened an interdisciplinary symposium to discuss the story in some of its incarnations and to consider why it is both permanent and renewable. As the story of a chaste wife falsely accused, it is a story of a woman endangered by a lie or, more precisely, by the difficulty of making the truth known in a situation in which the acceptance of the lie is in the interest of powerful people. It is a story about lust, about authority and the abuse of authority and, crucially, about witnessing: about the power of telling and retelling. As a story of a woman told for her by people whose interests are not her own, it is a story about the relationship between narrative and control and about narrative as control over life and death. For hundreds of years tellers and painters have shaped and reshaped its ends to their own purposes.

There is certainly some justification for reducing the various ethical, philosophical and artistic visions and revisions of the Susanna story to the standard Foucauldian assertion: life is a war. It's not a conversation nor a journey, but a pitched battle in which the best weapons are in the hands of the worst men. The powerful will generally be successful in taking the honest captive, demonstrating that not only does honesty not insure worldly success, it seems almost to guarantee victimization.

But surely the reason the story is so frequently retold and so perennially renewable is that most versions of the story actually deny this anxious (not to say paranoid) view of the world. Indeed, the bullies don't triumph; the story stealers (with occasional exceptions) don't get away with the goods. The *deus ex machina* provides not only redemption but knowledge. The truth is discovered and Susanna is returned to her family. Divine intervention at the last moment through the young prophet Daniel assures that truth embodied in a powerless and almost silent woman triumphs over worldly power.

The narrative skeleton of the Susanna story articulates the crucial thematic

1

and moral transformation of the divine comedy, if not of all comedy: the meek shall inherit the earth. Recently, post-structuralist critics have thoroughly documented the heretofore opaque truth about the reversibility of hierarchies, revealing the instabilities of power. They have also been astoundingly successful at producing strategies by means of which even undergraduates can be cultural terrorists, reconnoitering and besieging the city walls behind which received values thrive. But the history of the Susanna story reminds us that there have always been transformations, revolutions, upheavals, and paradigm-changing revelations. There have always been genres in which the hegemonies of value were conventionally dismantled in favor of the underdog, or in favor of the disenfranchised majority as against a powerful establishment. In folktales, children defeat witches and wolves; in the pastoral, beauty and sensual pleasure naturally prove superior to the over-schooled - to those who, like the elders, rely on intellectual tricks such as loopholes in the law - to achieve unethical aims. The Jewish hermeneutic tradition provides at least three genres in which right and might are not identical. The prophetic tradition (subsuming moralized history of the kind found in the books of Samuel for example) is virtually defined by the paradox that those who speak the truth will be ignored but will prove to have been true visionaries. The hasidic tradition (partly folk, partly prophetic) again identified intellectual underachievement with natural honesty, and awarded the ultimate triumph to the simple but pure soul. The tradition of Talmud Torah, of the learning of the law itself, explicitly includes the learning of the opposition views within it and also encompasses the genre of midrash aggada, a version of allegory that allows aspects of a story to be retold for new audiences or in changed historical circumstances. Christian parable and sacred history also provide generic possibilities by means of which apparently stable hierarchies can be reversed. The story of the resurrection itself is the paradigm here.

* * * * * * * *

The earliest extant version of the Susanna story is produced at a moment of great cultural instability. Written within the Hellenized Jewish community of Alexandria, no Hebrew or Aramaic version remains. The story was excluded from the Jewish canon, nor does early rabbinic literature make any mention of it. Yet Susanna's story was not only included in the Christian Bible, but she was, as Piero Boitani describes her, raised *in excelsis* in Christian Roman art and architecture, as part of the new religious community's struggle to define itself against its early Roman (pagan) persecutors. The story of Susanna's importance within the new Church derived, as several essays here point out, from its power as a parable, and as a promise of the possibility of transformation. Boitani shows, for example, how Christian art, namely, paintings in the Roman catacombs used for burial in the third and fourth centuries, figure Susanna as a symbol of the resurrection. This identification of Susanna with Jesus was made explicit in textual interpretation as well. She is, later on, understood as the prototype of the Christian martyr, "hemmed in on every side." All these Susannas are identified with transmutation: the dead will live, the scorned will be crowned.

Betsy Halpern-Amaru's essay, "Susanna's Journey Among the Church Fathers," expands the story of Susanna's journey by detailing the history of early Christian exegesis. According to Halpern-Amaru, the story of a Jewish woman who is the victim of an ill-functioning judicial system is retold and dejudaized for the purpose of authenticating the young church as both the legitimate heir and replacement of the old religion. Harold Fisch, in his reply to Boitani, suggests that the rabbis who excluded the story of Susanna from the canon may have done so because they understood it to be a midrash (on the *Song of Songs*, he argues) and not history. Fisch suggests that the artistic elegance of the text might itself have been enough to discourage the rabbis from canonizing it. He asks if it might not be the very silence of the Jewish interpreters that made the story attractive to the early Christian exegetes: the story of Susanna was available with the "commanding priority of its Hebrew origin," but, conveniently, without an original semitic text of any Jewish exegetic tradition.

Susan Sered and Samuel Cooper bring an anthropological perspective to their description of the apocryphal text as a mythic or folkloric text. In "Sexuality and Social Control," they describe the role of Daniel in the story as a version of the motif of the outsider who can say and do what an insider cannot. From the story's impure alignments of structural properties, they argue that it might have functioned to perform a transformation between cultural realms - say, between the biblical world in which women had no structural power within the patriarchy and a Christian world in which their voices began to be heard as morally powerful.

A second group of essays examines a variety of texts within a variety of historical contexts, in which, under different generic guises, Susanna is called upon to testify to whatever cultural/ideological transformation was advocated by the poet, dramatist, painter, or songwriter. David Lyle Jeffrey introduces us to a Middle English poem, the *Pistel of Swete Susan*, which he reads as Wycliffite polemic. He describes the context of the poem's composition (in the late fourteenth century) as one in which the Wycliffites would have felt themselves subjected to oppression by false witnesses who scrupled not at the unjust use of evidence. The text, according to Jeffrey, is a moral history: it is a protest and also a prophesy of the eventual undoing of false judges. The Wycliffite reformers thereby revived the earliest Jewish concerns of the text (if those are indeed to be found in the Old Greek version), namely the communal concern for the maintenance of an honest legal system.

M. Lindsay Kaplan's study of the Elizabethan morality play, the *Comedy of the Most Virtuous and Godly Susanna* (1578), "Sexual Slander and the Politics of the Erotic in Garter's *Susanna*," understands the author to have

conceived Susanna as a representative of the virtuous Protestants of England
beset by the red-robed Catholic bishops, even of the Queen herself, the
unmarried Elizabeth. Kaplan points out that for all her popularity Queen
Elizabeth was not immune to the fate of many Elizabethan women of high and
middle status: those who sought to attack her did so by means of sexual slander.
Kaplan resists Garter's generic claim to have produced a comedy, arguing for
the presence of a darker level of meaning: "the play resonates with the
uncertainty with which Elizabeth's supporters defended and championed her
cause."

Another resisting reader is Eleonore Stump who reads the apocryphal text
as a philosophical exemplum from which we can even now learn ethical lessons.
She asks how two old men whose collusion begins with common lust could
"move progressively towards the real wickedness of judicial murder?" Daniel's
heroism is mere cleverness, but Susanna, on Stump's reading, possesses the real
wisdom from which genuine martyrs are made. Ignoring the ending in which
Susanna is rewarded rather than martyred, and in which her salvation comes at
the hands of the young man, Daniel, Stump uses an analysis of behavior
suggested by Aquinas' theory of the interaction of will and intellect to chart the
descent of the Elders. The triumph of the clear-sighted and absolute Susanna
is in her moral stance, not her escape from judicial death on a technicality, as
it were. By doing so, Stump shows Nietzsche's suspicions about the
reversibility of hierarchies to be well founded; if the Christian comedy
embodied in folktale and prophesy shows the intervention of God on the side of
right, the Christian tragedy as studied by Aquinas reveals the less appetizing
possibility of transformation in the other direction. If the weak can find the
strength to resist evil, it is also true that trusted and presumably learned elders
can be thoroughly corrupted.

My own study of some of the sixteenth and seventeenth-century paintings
of Susanna and the Elders must also be considered resisting, but I am a resisting
viewer. Were I a man I suppose it would be harder to resist the beauty of
Susanna, almost always naked in a bath, or if not actually naked then pulling
off her clothes, or having them pulled off by the old men. But I am not the
intended viewer of these pictures. Is it, then, cranky of me to call attention to
the fact that there is no "bathing scene" in either version of the apocryphal
story, nor does Susanna ever appear undressed before her trial? It may be true
that a vision of a naked woman in her bath pops into every male mind who
reads about her plans for one, but surely it is not only women who would
protest against the painters' abandonment of the complexity of the moral issues,
and their betrayal of the virtuous Susanna for their own and their viewers'
pleasure. I will, as you will see, attribute the distortion of the paintings to their
association with the pastoral genre, learned apparently from their Greek context.

Sharon Baris' paper, "Hosannas to an American Susanna" changes the key
of the collection by asking us to listen as well as to read a set of transformations
of the Susanna story from the treasury of American literature surprisingly rich

in Susannas, Susyannas, and Daniels. According to Baris, the new world's revolutions are fought, above all, for the right to have one's voice heard. Baris' paper is a change from those preceding it that emphasize Susanna's silence. For Baris, Susanna's power, indeed the power of the new America, lies precisely in the ability to cry out in the insistence that the multiplicity of voices not be reduced to a single manifest destiny.

In sum, the essays collected here recognize the power of the text, the cry, the word, to authorize or withhold authority, as in the issues of canonization and the legitimation of new religious groups and new interpretations. They explore the power of the individual voice to witness or to slander, to prophesy or to pray. Finally they exhibit the possibilities of transformation, the effects of translation, and the different kinds of witness different versions provide. If the past is any guide, this set of judgments on Susanna and the Elders is no more than a progress report. You'll be seeing and hearing more of them.

Jerusalem, 1996

Susanna in Excelsis[1]

Piero Boitani
The University of Rome - Sapienza

This is the account of the progressive elevation of Susanna in Rome. Wherever and whenever the Susanna story originates, one thing is certain -- that by the beginning of the third century of our era it has reached the capital of the empire and become rather popular there among Christians. This is, as far as we know, the first time the tale of Susanna becomes a subject of Western art -- painting and sculpture -- and an important topic of theological, exegetical, and political debate. Does this encounter between myth, representation and history have a special meaning? In what particular way does it take place?

Appropriately, this story of a *gradus ad excelsa* begins underground. It is here, in those endless mazes of tunnels later known as catacombs, and excavated by Christians in the tufa -- the soft yellowish-brownish clay which makes up the soil of Rome -- that Susanna enters the Western *imaginaire*. The début is quite impressive, since paintings of the third and fourth centuries portraying her figure and her story are still extant in all the catacombs that,

---

[1] The title of this essay derives from the singular mistake Romans ignorant of Latin made during the Roman Catholic Mass when chanting the *Sanctus*. Instead of saying, "Hosanna in excelsis", they triumphantly proclaimed -- I have heard them with my own ears when I was a boy -- "Susanna in excelsis". Of course, the title is also meant to foreshadow the theme and texture of the essay, which is the progressive elevation of Susanna in the city of Rome.

In his "Peter Quince at the Clavier", Wallace Stevens significantly associates Susanna with Hosanna: "And thus it is that what I feel, / Here in this room, desiring you, / ...Is music. It is like the strain / Waked in the elders by Susanna....The red-eyed elders watching, felt / The basses of their beings throb / In witching chords, and their thin blood / Pulse pizzicati of Hosanna.

On the Susanna theme, see the following essential bibliography: W. Baumgartner, *Zum Alten Testament und seiner Umwelt* (Leiden, 1959), 42-67; E. Kirschbaum, ed., *Lexicon der christlichen Ikonographie* (Rome-Freiburg-Basel-Vienna), s.v. "Susanna"; A. Miskimin, ed., *Susannah: An Alliterative Poem of the Fourteenth Century* (New Haven-London, 1969), 189-99; S.C. Walker, *Seven Ways of Looking at Susanna* (Provo, Utah, 1984).

7

outside the walls, surround the city from northeast to south as if it were in a series of extensive webs clustering along the main highways.[2]

The oldest surviving instance, from the second half of the third century, is the lefthand side of the *arcosolium* vault in the St. Eusebius crypt at the catacombs of Callistus on the Appian Way, the Roman catacombs *par excellence*. In this scene, which earlier interpreters read -- significantly, as we shall see -- as the "judgement of a martyr", we have only one episode of the Susanna story. An adolescent standing on a stool addresses three figures, two men and a woman. The latter wears a long tunic which will become typical and has been identified as Susanna. The former is young Daniel. One of the two elders seems to be leaving in a downcast mood, while the other is receiving his sentence right on the spot. Clearly, what is essential here is the moral message of the story: virtue rewarded, vice punished, human justice exposed, divine Justice firmly established.

The second surviving instance of the Susanna story in Rome, from about a century later, is much more articulate -- it is in fact a piece of <u>narrative</u> found in the so-called Cappella greca, or Greek Chapel, in the catacombs of Priscilla on the Via Salaria. Here, the two walls of the nave are decorated with four episodes of the Susanna story. On the righthand side, two separate moments: the seduction attempt, and Daniel getting ready to defend Susanna from the accusation. Susanna stands at the center, taller than any other figure, wearing a sleeveless long tunic and, over it, a mantle which forms a hood on her head. Her arms are stretched out and up to eye level as in prayer. To her left, Daniel lifts with his left hand the hem of his cloak, keeping the right underneath it. The two elders come in from the other side, elbow to elbow, illustrating verses 19-20 in Theodotion: "When the maids had gone out, the two elders rose and ran to her, and said: 'Look, the garden doors are shut, no one sees us, and we are in love with you; so give your consent, and lie with us'".[3] In the fresco, each keeps his right hand stretched out before him, rushing towards Susanna as

---

[2] See H. Leclercq, "Suzanne", in F. Cabrol et H. Leclercq, *Dictionnaire d'Archéologie Chrétienne et de Liturgie*, vol. XV (Paris, 1953); J. Wilpert, *Le pitture delle catacombe romane* (Rome, 1903); L. Hertling and E. Kirschbaum, The Roman Catacombs and their Martyrs (London, 1960). Besides those I briefly discuss here, other representations of the Susanna story are to be found in the catacombs of Domitilla (Appian Way area), Saints Marcellinus and Peter (Via Casilina), and of the *Coemeterium Maius* (Via Nomentana) -- all fourth century. The section of the mosaic representing Susanna in the fourth-century Roman church of St. Costanza (next to the church and catacombs of St. Agnes on the Via Nomentana) is now lost, although ancient copies of it survive. See E. Michel, *Die Mosaiken von S. Costanza in Rom* (Leipzig, 1912).

[3] All quotations from the Susanna episode in this essay are from Theodotion's Greek version (which is the one used by Hippolytus), as printed with the *Septuaginta*, ed. A. Rahlfs (Stuttgart, 1935) at the beginning of the Book of Daniel. The English translations are mine, based on that of *Daniel, Esther, and Jeremiah: The Additions*, ed. C.A. Moore, Anchor Bible 44 (Garden City, N.J., 1977), and that of *The Oxford Annotated Bible with the Apocrypha*, eds. H.G. May and B.M. Metzger (New York, 1965).

if striving to reach her first. One is marginally ahead of the other and turns to his companion. The latter has his eyes fixed on the lady.

The story continues on the opposite wall with two more episodes. The first illustrates verses 34-35 of Theodotion: "Then the two elders stood up in the midst of the people, and laid their hands upon her head. And she, weeping, looked up toward heaven, for her heart trusted in the Lord". In the fresco, they stand to the left and right of Susanna, laying one hand each on her hooded head while each seizes one of her arms with the other. Separated from this group by a small tree, a man and a woman, the latter veiled, are praying with their arms stretched out as if to thank God for delivering Susanna from the false accusation. Although, following Theodotion 63, these could represent Hilkiah and his wife, or even Joakim and Susanna, they almost certainly are Daniel and Susanna.

Clearly, what interests the painter here is to organize the narrative not in chronological sequence, but by pairing and contrasting different moments. On each wall we have an early and a late stage of the story, and on each wall the main opposition is between a static and a dynamic scene. In the latter, movement conveys passion and violence; in the former, stillness indicates dignity and conformity to God's will. Ultimately, the contrast is summed up in the opposite movements of the characters' arms: those of Susanna and Daniel are always stretched and lifted in the typical position of prayer, those of the elders seek to touch the woman and consecrate dominion on her by laying hands on her head. By grabbing and pinning down Susanna's arms, the two elders effectively bind her and break her prayer posture. This, however, is triumphantly resumed in the same picture, at the chronological end of the story. If one were to express the basic contrast of the two frescoes in one sentence, one would say that they represent the struggle of coercion against prayer.

Archaeologists and iconologists have identified at least four more Susanna paintings (all from the fourth century) in the Roman catacombs. Each represents only one scene of the story, thus neglecting the diachronic or narrative dimension which is so prominent in Priscilla and returning to the monothematic formulation we have seen in Callistus. I choose one for purposes that will become clear presently. This appears on the front wall of the Celerina *arcosolium* in the catacombs of Praetextatus, also in the area of the Appian Way. Here, mimesis itself (let alone narrative) has disappeared, replaced by symbolism. A lamb occupies the center of the picture, surrounded on either side by a wolf. Above the wolf on the right hand side, the word SENIORIS makes clear that this is one of the two elders, whilst the name, SVSANNA, is visible above the lamb. "Violence and lust lay a trap for innocent purity" clearly is the primary message of the fresco -- a simple, straightforward moral reading of the Susanna story. But for any Christian the lamb would also obviously recall Christ, the paschal victim, and (following Revelation 21. 9-10) the bridegroom of the heavenly Jerusalem, i.e., of the Church. In a more historico-political perspective, the wolves could then stand, according to

Matthew 7. 15, for the false prophets against whom Jesus warns his disciples (the heretics threatening the integrity of the Church), or, following traditional interpretations of Matthew 10. 15 and Luke 10. 3 -- "I send you forth as lambs among wolves" -- for the Jews and Pagans let loose against the faithful. In other words, the Susanna story has left the realm of narrative to enter that of morality and interpretation. In less than two hundred years it has become a sign, suspended as it were between symbolism and allegory.

I shall soon return to this important metamorphosis. But in order to understand it we have, I think, to ask a preliminary question. Why are paintings of Susanna so frequent in the catacombs? Catacombs are burial grounds, and pictorial decoration, though not uncommon, is not exactly extensive in early Christian graveyards. It normally is to be found only in the chapels where the faithful would assemble to commemorate the departed and the martyrs and around the most important tombs. Furthermore, the subjects of these paintings are fairly limited: apart from the symbolic peacock, dove, fish, and anchor, Old Testament scenes (which in the period before Constantine outnumber the New Testament ones) portray Adam and Eve, Noah's ark, the sacrifice of Isaac, Moses striking water from the rock, Jonah and the whale, the three young men in the burning furnace, Daniel in the lions' den. Why, then, Susanna and the elders? Early Christians don't seem to be interested in the legal aspects that might fascinate readers of the Septuagint, nor in the sexual itch the story will prompt in the Renaissance, nor finally in the detective plot that would appeal to us. Why do they find the story so relevant to their concerns as to have it sculpted, too, again and again on their sarcophagi -- four at least in Rome alone?[4]

The answer brings us to ideas of salvation or survival, personal on the one hand, political on the other. Susanna has to do with death, the single crucial event of human life -- with death and resurrection. She is indeed condemned to death by the people, and cries out with a loud voice, in Theodotion's version (42), "καὶ ἰδοὺ ἀποθνήσκω" ("*kài idoù apothnésko*"): literally, "and behold, I die". She is, however, rescued from death by Daniel, or rather by God, "who saves those who hope in him" (Theodotion, 60), through Daniel. The Savior vanquishes death, Susanna is risen. In fact,

---

[4] See H. Leclercq, "Suzanne", op. cit., 1748-9; J. Wilpert, *I sarcofagi cristiani antichi* (Rome, 1929). The four Roman sarcophagi are in the Museum of the Campo Santo Teutonico in the Vatican (six scenes), in the Roman National Museum (Diocletian's Baths), and two in the Lateran Museum (now part of the Vatican Museum). Susanna episodes are to be found on sarcophagi in Arles (*Musée d'art chrétien*), Narbonne (*Musée Lamourguier*), and Gerona (Church of S. Felice). These go back to the late third and the following century. Other early representations of Susanna in glass cups: at *Homblières* (4th century), Podgoritza (9th century, now in St. Petersburg), the British Museum (the crystal cup of Lothar II, 9th century, which confirms the theory presented here of the relationship between story, politics and history). Finally, there is an ivory box (ascribed to the fourth century) in Brescia with three scenes of the Susanna story.

Susanna's association with death is neither merely verbal nor purely metaphorical, but also liturgical. In the *Ordo Commendationis animae quando infirmus est in extremis* -- the Prayer ordained for the sick in *extremis* which apparently goes back to the period between the third and fourth centuries -- the example of Susanna was presented to the dying faithful as one of the reasons for their trust in God's mercy. After a long litany beginning with the iterated acclamation, Κύριε ἐλέησον, Χρίστε ἐλέησον (*Kyrie elèison, Christe elèison*) (Lord, have mercy; Christ, have mercy), one would say: *Suscipe, Domine, servum tuum in locum sperandae sibi salvationis a misericordia tua* (Lord, receive your servant in the place where he hopes to have salvation through your mercy), and, within a list which includes Enoch and Elijah, Noah, Abraham, Job, Isaac, Lot, Moses, Daniel (*Libera, Domine, animam ejus, sicut liberasti Danielem de lacu leonum*), David, the three Jews, Peter and Paul, and the virgin Thecla, one would say: *Libera, Domine, animam ejus, sicut liberasti Susannam de falso crimine* (Lord, free his soul as you freed Susanna from her false crime).[5] Thus, Susanna (like Daniel freed from the lions' den) typologically signifies the soul of every Christian. By evoking her at the hour of death Christians voice their hope of the soul's survival and salvation. One could hardly imagine a stronger reason for the Christians' attachment to the story of our heroine. Nor is it any longer difficult to understand why she is so often portrayed in those places where the bodies of the faithful rest and rot -- catacombs and sarcophagi.

Yet the destiny of Susanna is not just that of meeting and overcoming individual death -- a high enough elevation *ad excelsa*. By coming to Rome between the second and third centuries she enters history and becomes the paradigm of Christianity's survival as an organized body of individuals, in short as an *ecclesia*, a Church. In fact, I would go as far as to say that the fifty years which comprise the last two decades of the second and the first three of the third century constitute a true "age of Susanna".

Perhaps the best way of proving this assertion is to look at the work of Hippolytus and at the context in which it develops. Hippolytus was an important personality among the Roman presbyters during the first decades of the third century: when Origen came to Rome around 212 he attended one of his sermons. Hippolytus refused to accept the teaching of the bishop of Rome, Zephyrinus (198-217), and under his successor, Callistus (217-222), whom he rejected as a heretic, he seems to have set himself up as an "anti-Pope". However, he must have enjoyed high reputation in the city, for a statue of him with a list of his writings was erected in some public place probably during his own lifetime. His works, all in Greek, include a *Philosophoumena* or *Refutation of all Heresies*, treatises on the nature of the universe against Noetus

---

[5] See H. Leclercq, "Suzanne" and "Défunts", in *Dictionnaire*, op. cit.; J.H. Srawley, *The Early History of the Liturgy*, 2nd ed. (London, 1947); J.A. Jungmann, *The Early Liturgy to the Time of Gregory the Great* (London, 1961).

and Plato, on the *Apostolic Tradition*, on God and the resurrection of the flesh (addressed to Julia Mammaea, mother of the emperor Alexander Severus), on the Antichrist, a *Commentary on the Song of Songs*, a *Commentary on the Psalms*, and a *Commentary on Daniel*.[6]

In this latter work Hippolytus takes a decisive political stance. Up until then interpretation of the Books of Revelation and of Daniel had been combined by exegetes. For instance, Irenaeus of Lyons, whose disciple Hippolytus is sometimes supposed to have been, had maintained that the last of the four beasts of Daniel was the image of the Roman empire, which would be divided amongst ten kings. Its "little horn" prefigured Antichrist, which was also foreshadowed by the "beast out of the sea" of Revelation. Yet Irenaeus, who lived in the period of the "great waiting" for the end of time attested by the Muratorian Canon, still believes that the practical attitude Christians should have towards the Empire ought to be dictated by the Pauline λόγιον (*logion*), "*non est potestas nisi a Deo*; the powers that be are ordained by God".[7]

Hippolytus, on the other hand, goes much further. In Discourse IV, chapter ix of his *Commentary on Daniel* he writes that the Roman empire κρατεῖ κατ' ἐνέργειαν τοῦ σατανᾶ (*kratèi kat'enérgeian tou satanà*), rules through (or, according to) the power of Satan. It is, he says, a counterfeit of Christianity because, unlike the Babylonian, Persian and Greek empires, it represents not one nation but a sum of nations united for the sake of war. Hence, it is inevitably destined to die. Since the world was made to last six thousand years and Christ was born five thousand five hundred years after the Creation, Rome will die in the year 500 A.D., its empire divided "according to nations" by ten kings, then re-united by Antichrist, and finally destroyed by the divine παρουσία (*parousia*) in the Second Coming.

It is in the context of this prophecy -- a singularly accurate one as to the date and the way of Rome's fall -- that Hippolytus looks at past and present circumstances. When he comes to comment on the Susanna story (I, xii), he rearranges, first of all, the genealogy of Jesus constructed by Matthew (1. 1) so as to make the issue of Levi and that of Judah join in Susanna and in Christ. He thus rewrites the past in the following fanciful manner: Susanna was the daughter of Hilkiah, the priest who found the book of the Law in the house of the Lord when King Josiah ordered the Holy of Holies to be purified (II Kings 22. 10; II Chron. 34. 14). She was the sister of the prophet Jeremiah (whose father's name was Hilkiah). Her husband Joakim (rather than Matthew's

---

[6] All references to, and quotations from Hippolytus's Daniel commentary are to the text of the *Commentaire sur Daniel* edited by M. Lefèvre (Paris, 1947). The sections which have survived in the Greek original have been checked against *Hippolytus Werke*, Ier Band, *Exegetische und homiletische Schriften*, eds. G.N. Bonwetsch and H. Achelis (Leipzig, 1897) and Migne, *Patrologia Graeca* 10, 261-962.

[7] (Romans 1. 13, 1 ff.) Significantly, this document makes the canon of the New Testament (the earliest we have) coincide with the *finis temporum* in which it was redacted -- an age preceded by those of the prophets and the apostles.

Jechonias) was one of King Josiah's five sons, and thus priesthood, prophecy and monarchy are joined by the marriage of Joakim and Susanna; of them was born Jechonias, and from him Matthew's line of descent can start all over again and culminate with Jesus.

What interests Hippolytus here is not just the correcting of Matthew's notoriously problematic genealogy. He is aiming at -- indirectly perhaps -- a figural parallel between Susanna and Jesus, who share the same "messianic" ancestry. This is confirmed later on (xxvii) when Hippolytus draws the parallel between Daniel's words, "I am innocent of the blood of this woman" (Thedotion, 46), and those of Pilate in Matthew's gospel (27. 24), "I am innocent of the blood of this just person". Susanna is indeed being elevated to the highest.

But concern for the past never is Hippolytus' main preoccupation: as with all Christian authors from the time of the evangelists, for him the past is instrumental -- a means of speaking about the present. And the present is the cultural and political reality of Christianity. For example, Hippolytus prefaces his discussion of the Susanna story with two quick allusions to the question of its canonicity. He asks himself (xiii) "why people in captivity and servants to the Babylonians could meet in one place as free persons", and answers that, after deporting them, Nebuchadnezzar treated them humanely, allowing them to meet so that they could do whatever the Law demanded. He then adds (xiv) that "the chiefs of the Jews want to take this story out of Scripture, claiming that nothing of the sort ever took place in Babylon, because they are ashamed of what the elders did at that time". "They", he concludes, "do not recognize in it the divine plan *οἰκονομία* (*oikonomía*) of the Father".

Question, answer, and explanation repeat (or anticipate) the argument between Julius Africanus and Origen about the canonicity of the Susanna episode.[8] Origen firmly believed (though he apparently admitted to some doubts in his *Stromateis*) that Susanna was a true part of the Book of Daniel, since it was contained in both the Septuagint and Theodotion. Moreover, the story showed up the Jewish elders in an unhappy light, so that the Synagogue had obvious reasons for suppressing it. Origen's view, however, was challenged in a letter by Julius Africanus -- a Palestinian who became chief librarian of the Roman emperor Alexander Severus. He maintained that the famous verbal pun in verses 54 ff., being possible only in Greek, proves the story of Susanna to be an addition to the original Book of Daniel.[9] Origen

---

[8] The whole argument, with Africanus' letter and Origen's reply, in Migne, *Patrologia Graeca* 11, 42 ff.

[9] The wordplay occurs, in both the Septuagint and Theodotion, when Daniel interrogates the two elders separately, asking each of them under which tree he saw Susanna and the young man being intimate with each other. The first elder answers, "under a mastic tree" *σχῖνον* (*skhinon*). Daniel replies: "...the angel of God...will cut *σχίσει* (*skhisei*) you in two". The second elder's answer is, "under an evergreen oak" *πρῖνον* (*prinon*). Daniel says: "...the angel of God is waiting with his sword to saw *πρίσαι* (*prisai*) you in two..." The *Oxford*

replied that the pun could have been introduced by the translators, but that did not prove that there was no Hebrew original.

Origen, Julius Africanus, Hippolytus: it is through Rome that Susanna becomes a hot cultural issue. The court of the Roman emperor works as a great catalyst. Alexander Severus' mother, Julia Mammaea, is pro-Christian, and summons Origen to Antioch for a discussion. Hippolytus addresses to her his treatise on the resurrection of the flesh. The emperor himself keeps statues of Apollonius of Tyana, Orpheus, Abraham and Christ in his *lararium* or private chapel.[10]

Hippolytus' *Commentary*, however, is there to testify that questions of philology and canon are never neutral, that in fact they always have a highly political significance. The chiefs of Israel, he writes, do not recognize in the Susanna story the *oikonomìa* of the Father. For him, this "economy" is neither literary nor merely moral. It is historical. "Susanna", he continues, "had to suffer from the elders what one still has to suffer from the princes of Babylon. She was the figure of the Church, her husband Joakim that of Christ. The garden adjoining his house figured the society of saints, planted like fruitful trees amidst the Church. Babylon is the world. The two elders represent the two people who conspire against the Church, that of Circumcision and that of the Gentiles".

We are brought back to the symbolic fresco in the catacombs of Praetextatus. In Hippolytus' *Commentary*, the allegory has both the swell of the great waves of history and the dramatic urgency of the present political situation. Susanna, he maintains (xvi), is a prefiguration in the sense Paul gives to the word: "Now all these things happened to them in figure: and they are written for our correction, upon whom the ends of the world are come".[11] Joakim's garden -- that garden where Susanna has a bath which means the baptism of the Church, administered on Easter Sunday by the two maids of Faith and Charity and accompanied by the oil of the Spirit and the cosmetics, i.e., the commandments of the Word -- is the earthly correlative of the Garden of Eden. And this, in turn, is the figure or "model" of the true garden, the Church. The Church is "the spiritual garden of God planted on Christ as if eastward, where one sees all kinds of trees: the issue of the patriarchs who died in the beginning, the works of the prophets accomplished after the Law, the chorus of the Apostles who had their wisdom from the Word, the chorus of the Martyrs saved by the blood of Christ, the theory of the Virgins sanctified by water, the chorus of the Doctors, the order of Bishops, Priests and Levites". In this grand vision, the *Ecclesia* is built up by successive historical stages, in

---

Annotated Bible with the Apocrypha has by far the best suggestion I know to translate the pun into English: "Under a clove tree...the angel will cleave you"; "under a yew tree...the angel will hew you asunder".

[10] *Historia Augusta*, 29, 2. The reliability of the *Historia* has been questioned.

[11] I Corinthians 10, 11: Douai-Rheims version.

a liturgical procession, a sequence, a litany, as if it were in a truly Roman concretion of different epochs and different orders. This is the "economy" of the Father; this is Susanna. In purity, she is the female equivalent of Jacob's son, Joseph (xxii). She stands at the beginning of human time, prefigured by Eve (xviii), and at the center of time, as the "spouse of Christ".

But the enemy lies in wait for her now, as Hippolytus works on his *Commentary*. For him as for the painter of the Susanna allegory in the catacombs of Praetextatus, the "lying seductors" are those who "pervert by means of their heretical teachings" (xxii). Alternatively, they represent external adversaries. Daniel, Hippolytus writes, speaks to one of the elders as to a man "learned in the Law"; he calls the other "offspring of Canaan and not of Judah".[12] He obviously means, Hippolytus says (xxix), that the former stands for the Jews and the latter for the Pagans. "The two people, prompted by Satan who acts in them, never cease to meditate persecutions and tribulations against the Church", often misunderstanding each other (xv). But "when they agree", then their attack against the Church is subtle and sudden:

> They spy for the opportune day and, penetrating as intruders into the house of the Lord, when all pray and sing hymns to God, they seize a few people and drag them outside and do violence to them, saying: "Come on, have commerce with us and honour the gods. Otherwise, we will testify against you".[13] And as these do not consent, they bring them before the tribunal and accuse them of acting against Caesar's decree and have them condemned to death (xx).

This has all the urgency of a contemporary scene. It "happens today", Hippolytus writes. "When the saints are arrested and dragged to court, the crowd gets together to see what is going on" (xxv). Their enemies start shouting: "Dispatch them from the earth, the people of this kind. They must not live" (xxiii). "*Christianos ad leonem!*" (Christians to the lions!), as Tertullian, an older contemporary of Hippolytus, reports.[14] In 202 Septimius Severus had promulgated his edict against Jews and Christians. It was not always enforced, and in 212 Tertullian calls Septimius Severus "Christianorum memor" and says that his successor, Caracalla, was brought up "lacte Christiano", on Christian milk. But it was always possible to accuse someone of being a Christian and denounce him or her to the authorities. If the judge was a traditionalist, a Pagan, the Christian would be convicted on the basis of the edict and condemned.[15]

---

[12] Hippolytus is quoting Theodotion, 52-3 and 56.

[13] Theodotion, 21.

[14] *Apologeticus*, 40, 2.

[15] The best reconstruction of this historical period and of Callistus' story is S. Mazzarino's in his *L'impero romano*, vol. II (Rome-Bari, 1973), 451-90. See also H. Chadwick, *The Early Church* (Harmondsworth, 1967), 84-113.

Something similar had in fact happened before Septimius Severus' reign to Callistus, whose story we have from his great opponent, Hippolytus himself. Callistus was a slave and a Christian. His master, Carpophorus, was a Christian freedman of Commodus' imperial household. Carpophorus appointed his slave as head of his own private bank, a bank which made good profits by getting money from Christians and lending it to non-Christians at high interest rates. Yet at one point Callistus and his bank went bankrupt, perhaps because some Jews failed to refund a huge loan they had received. Carpophorus threw his manager into the "pistrinum", the living hell where slaves were forced to turn the millstone. Freed from it shortly afterwards, Callistus disturbed a Jewish religious ceremony on a Saturday. The Jews beat him up and accused him of being a Christian before the tribunal of the city prefect. Although the powerful Carpophorus denied it, Callistus confessed he was indeed a Christian. The prefect, a "schoolfellow" of the emperor Marcus Aurelius, was a strict pagan. He condemned Callistus to the Sardinian mines. The two elders had in fact conspired against Susanna.

The story's sequel is also fascinating. Marcia, the emperor Commodus' concubine, was *theophilés*, God fearing. She succeeded in getting Callistus out of the Sardinian mines. He returned to Rome, where the bishop, Victor, gave him a monthly cheque and sent him to Anzio. Victor's successor, Zephyrinus, called him back to the City and appointed him "curator" of Rome's most famous Christian graveyard, which was eventually named after him: the catacombs of Callistus on the Appian Way. When Zephyrinus died, Callistus was, to Hippolytus' great dismay, elected "Pope".

The oldest surviving pictorial representation of Susanna and the elders, it will be remembered, appears in the crypt of St. Eusebius at the catacombs of Callistus. This, then, is how a story becomes history and how history turns into painting. In this double metamorphosis, exegesis works both outside and inside. On the one hand, it acts as a reagent, a substance employed in chemistry as a test to determine the presence of some other substance by means of the reaction which is produced: it allows us to observe the change from our external point of view, prompting our own interpretation of the phenomenon -- of words, pictures, and events. On the other, as an agent, exegesis precipitates the transformation itself. It operates on events, shaping them into words and pictures.

But it does not just do that. It also changes words and pictures into new events, it makes stories happen. The Roman Church has always possessed an extraordinary ability in this respect. When the elders force Susanna to decide whether to lie with them or be accused of adultery, she sighs deeply, saying: "I am hemmed in on every side. For if I do this thing, it is death for me; and if I do not, I shall not escape your hands".[16] Hippolytus interprets these words as expressing the anguish of the Christian martyr. "Those", he writes (xxi),

---

[16] Theodotion, 22.

"who are arrested because of Christ's name, if they do what men command to them, die to God and live for the world; if they do not do it, they cannot escape the hands of the judges, but are condemned by them and die".

It did not take long for the Roman Church to transform this piece of exegesis into a story, a canon, and history. Diocletian became emperor in 284, fifty years after Alexander Severus' death. He reigned until 305, having divided the empire into East and West, with two Augusti and two Caesars to rule each section, and having started in 303 the last great wave of persecutions against the Church before Costantine made the empire itself Christian in 313.

The bishop of Rome between 283 and 296 was Caius. His brother Gabinius, a presbyter, had a daughter well-known both for her beauty and for her learning in "sacred letters". Her name was...Susanna. Diocletian decided she should become the wife of his partner in the empire, the Augustus Maximian. He therefore sent Claudius to ask for her. Susanna, "fortified by the Holy Ghost", refused, declaring before her father that she wanted to keep her chastity. Claudius, struck by her strength and instructed by Caius and Gabinius, became a Christian with all his family. A month and sixteen days later, Diocletian charged one of his retainers, Maximus, with enquiring what had happened to Claudius and Susanna. Maximus found Claudius "praying in a hairshirt". Awed by what he had seen, and taught by Caius and Gabinius, Maximus, too, was christened. Two weeks later, Diocletian learnt of these events. He sent another man, Julius, to punish Claudius and Maximus and imprison Susanna. The outcome is not known, but fifty five days later Diocletian ordered Susanna to be brought to his wife Serena, "who was secretly a Christian". The two women began to pray and sing Psalms. When this was reported to Diocletian, he decided that Susanna should be led back to her father's house either -- the sources are not quite clear on this point -- by his son Maximin or his partner Maximian. If it was the former, Diocletian instructed him to rape Susanna. But Maximin found her praying, an extraordinary light shining upon her, and returned to the emperor. Diocletian then dispatched a fourth man, Macedonius, to force Susanna to sacrifice to the gods. She resisted. Macedonius stripped her naked and whipped her, while she kept saying, "Gloria tibi, Domine" (Glory to you, Lord), until she was killed by his sword. Her body was collected by the empress Serena and buried near Diocletian's Baths.

This is the version printed in the *Acta Sanctorum* together with the critical emendations supplied by Cesare Baronius in his late sixteenth-century *Annales Ecclesiastici*.[17] It seems obvious that, whether or not there actually was a Roman martyr named Susanna, her story was invented (in all likelihood, quite

---

[17] *Acta Sanctorum*, curantibus J.B. Sollerio, J. Pinio, G. Cupero, P. Boschio, ed. nov. cur. J. Carnandet, "Augusti Tomus Secundus" (Paris-Rome, 1867), *Die Undecima Augusti*, 624-632. See also V.L. Kennedy, *The Saints of the Canon of the Mass*, 2nd ed. (London, 1963); H. Delehaye, *The Legends of the Saints* (London, 1962).

some time after the events it purported to relate), and invented in order to create a Christian, Roman parallel to the old Susanna. The sexual innuendos in the legend are clear enough, as is the spying several people do on the virgin. Nor would I be surprised if a critic of functionalist inclinations were to maintain that in the Christian version Diocletian and Macedonius played a role somewhat akin to that of the two elders. Be that as it may, this is the way Susanna enters the Roman canon of saints -- the manner, that is, in which she is "translated" to the highest.

Perhaps because it settled down in Rome, the Catholic Church has always been rather thorough in its practices. In the Tridentine Mass for the Saturday after the third Quadragesima Sunday, in Lent, the first reading is the Susanna story from the Book of Daniel, the Gospel -- with impeccable figural cogency -- John's account of the woman taken in adultery. The station church, i.e., the church where the Pope would celebrate Mass on this particular day, is...the church of St. Susanna near the Baths of Diocletian.[18] Thus, as if this really were the "economy of the Father", story -- a double one by now -- returns to liturgy, and Susanna once more embodies the *Ecclesia*, a physical church of stone and marble.

The church was built as a basilica in the fourth century, rebuilt in 687, transformed in the ninth century (when Leo III apparently called a public Council there in Charlemagne's presence), restructured in the fifteenth century under Sixtus IV, and completely reshaped from 1595 to 1603 by Cardinal Girolamo Rusticucci in the context of Sixtus V's great new urban plan for that area of Rome -- a true example of Roman historical and artistic concretion. The architects called to work on it were Domenico Fontana and Carlo Maderno. Maderno, who a few years later designed the present front of St. Peter's, built for St. Susanna's what art historians consider as the prototype of all baroque façades.[19]

The program for the interior decoration was almost certainly inspired by Cardinal Cesare Baronius.[20] It began with the presbytery and the apse, where Cesare Nebbia and Tommaso Laureti painted the altar piece, the spherical vault of the apse, and the side walls with scenes from the story of St. Susanna. The nave and counterfaçade were decorated by the Bolognese painter Baldassarre Croce with six great frescoes. The theme: Susanna and the elders.

Thus, the stories of the two Susannas are definitively joined. Moving in history through the sediments of imagination, canonization and liturgy, the

---

[18] *Missale Romanum ex decreto sacrosancti Concilii Tridentini restitutum S. Pii V Pontificis Maximi jussu editum*...13th ed.(Turin-Rome, 1961), 100-102.

[19] For the history of the church, see R. Krautheimer, *Corpus basilicarum christianorum Romae* (Vatican City, 1937); A.M. Affanni, *Inquadramento urbanistico* and *Santa Susanna*, in *Santa Susanna e San Bernardo alle Terme* (Rome, 1993), 13-26.

[20] For the interior decoration, see R. Vodret, *La decorazione interna*, in *Santa Susanna e San Bernardo*, cit., 28-48; B. Apollonj Ghetti, *Le chiese di Roma illustrate. S. Susanna* (Rome, 1965).

double myth becomes architecture and painting. From the catacombs to a baroque basilica: the circle is completed, the ascent to the highest achieved. The apse of this church on the Quirinal hill in Rome shows us St. Susanna "in gloria."

The Journey of Susanna Among the Church Fathers

Betsy Halpern-Amaru

Vassar College

Some have viewed *Susanna and the Elders* as a literary response to the family tragedy of Shimon ben Shetah, the early Pharisee whose son was executed on the basis of perjured testimony.[1] Others have argued that the tale originated as an early form of the rabbinic legends that developed around the two false prophets, Ahab ben Kolaiah and Zedekiah ben Maaseiah, who "committed adultery with their neighbors' wives" (Jer 29:23).[2] More recently, it has been suggested that the story started as a secular folktale that, over the course of time, was thoroughly judaized.[3] Quite frankly, we cannot speak with

---

[1] See Nicholas Delange, *Apocrypha: Jewish Literature of the Hellenistic Age* (New York: Viking, 1978), 128 and André Lacocque, *The Feminine Unconventional, Four Subversive Figures in Israel's Tradition* (Minneapolis: Fortress, 1990), 24. The story of the perjury against and execution of Shimon ben Shetah's son appears in San. 6.3.

[2] In the version in b.San 93a the two seducers tell the daughter of Nebuchadnezzar that God has commanded the deed. The attempt is thwarted because she goes to her father who decides to put them to the test of a fiery furnace undergone by Hananniah, Mishael and Azariah. Hoping to exculpate themselves, the villains insist that Joshua the High Priest be joined with them so as to make it a test of three. The prophets burn, but the priest emerges with only his garments singed. With various thematic changes, the legend also appears in rabbinic Midrash. In *Pesiqta de R. Kahana* (24.15) the false prophets seduce "their neighbors' wives" with the promise they will give birth to a prophet son. The pregnant women come to Nebuchadnezzar's wife who reports the matter to her husband. In another version, the victims are Babylonian women, including Nebuchadnezzar's daughter and/or wife, and the villainy of the false prophets includes divination of the sex of the unborn child (*Tanhuma*, Vayikra 10; *Midrash Aggada II, Vayikra*). Origen and Jerome refer to the rabbinic legend in their discussions of Susanna (*Jerome, Commentary on Daniel*, 13.5.). The theory that the Jeremiah prophets provided the background for the Susanna story was first put forth by N. Brull, "Das apokryphische Susanna Buch" *Jahrbuch für judische Geschichte und Literatur* 3 (1877), 1-69.

[3] On the theory that the story originated as a secular folk tale, see Carey A. Moore, *Daniel, Esther and Jeremiah, The Additions*, Anchor Bible 44 (Garden City, NY: Doubleday, 1977), 88-89.

21

much certainty about the work until the second century B.C.E. when it appears in the Septuagint as the second of three additions to the biblical book of Daniel. Most probably based on a Semitic *Vorlage*,[4] this sparse text of approximately forty-one verses[5] is as close as we get to the initial formulation of the story. It is an important starting point for *Susanna and the Elders* which enters the Christian canon in a different form;[6] and for almost a millennium thereafter there is no Jewish expression of interest in, or even comment upon, Susanna's tale.

In the Old Greek version of the tale the central issues are neither lust and passion nor even piety and prophecy. Indeed, notably lacking in drama, the narrative is very specifically focused: the story line functions as little more than a case history illustration of corruption and bias within a traditional judicial system. The author does not develop any of the principle characters. Susanna, or "the Jewess" as she once is called, is heard only twice in direct voice (in refusal of the overture of the corrupt elderly judges and a second time in prayer); and her Joseph-like piety never becomes a central or controlling motif. We are told that she is the daughter of Hilkiah and married to one Joakim with whom she has four children (vv. 7, 30). A good looking woman (v. 7), she is refined (v. 31), pious (v. 35), and has not only the services, but also the loyalty, of five hundred servants (v. 30)! Clearly a female representative of the privileged class, she is accustomed to taking afternoon walks in the privacy of her husband's garden where, with no bathing intention whatsoever, she is accosted by the elder judges. But all this data is case relevant - circumstantial so to speak. Designed as victim par excellence, Susanna represents the danger to all, regardless of moral character or social position, in an ill functioning judicial system. Her attractive femininity and naiveté[7] are primary indicators of vulnerability; and her wealth and pious character extend the endangerment far beyond concern for the innocent, but spiritually and/or materially, underprivileged.

Male characters are similarly tactically devised. By virtue of both sex and age, the elder judges represent the socially empowered. Never dramatically

---

[4] Moore, 82-84.

[5] Since most editions favor the longer Theodotion version, when the original Old Greek narrative is presented, the verse numbers are coordinated with those of the Theodotion one.

[6] The Greek text of both versions of the story is found in Joseph Ziegler, ed., *Susanna, Daniel, Bel et Draco, Septuaginta: Vestus Testamentum Graecum* XVI.2 (Gottingen: Vandenhoeck and Ruprecht, 1954).

[7] The Old Greek version makes a point of her ignorance of the attraction she holds for the elders. I suspect that the parenthetical comment - "although the woman did not know of this matter" v. 10 - reflects the author's sensitivity to the implication that Susanna's beauty somehow makes her guilty of enticement. The phrasing of the preceding sentence - "...one did not admit to the other the evil which possessed them on account of her" - recalls the passage in the story of Sara and Abram's in Egypt when the Pharaoh, enticed by her beauty, takes Sara and "on account of her" (בעבורה), Abram thrives (Gen 12:10-16).

developed, their villainy seems almost mundane. They "averted their eyes, not looking to Heaven," and succumbed to wickedness, not once, but so repeatedly that it became their habit (v. 52). As for the young Daniel, his role is minimal. In spite of the celebration of youth at the end of story, the reader is quite aware that it is divine intervention, not Daniel's sagacity, that brings the narrative to resolution. The real hero, the only "character" that is transformed in the story, is the community that sits in judgment. Responsive to the interrogation of the witnesses (which, not insignificantly, forms the body of this narrative), the community corrects its traditional social biases and commits itself to an enlightened sense of justice. This transformation, albeit somewhat simplistic, is the central theme of the Alexandrian version of the moral fable. Yet when *Susanna and the Elders* enters the Christian canon and the exegetical tradition of the Church, the community justice motif is lost.

Perhaps as early as the next century[8] the story becomes the dramatic tale of beauty, passion, and piety that is so familiar in western art and literature. Extended to an indeterminate length (vv. 8, 12), the action takes place exclusively at the home of Susanna's wealthy husband, Joakim, now so preeminent that his personal residence, rather than the synagogue, houses the court. The roles and the emotions of the major characters in the drama are fully developed. Never explicitly identified as a Jewess, Susanna is described as "very beautiful," instructed in the Law, and god-fearing. She doesn't just walk in the garden; she elaborately prepares to bathe there; she doesn't just respond to the seducers, but groans, verbally acknowledges her dilemma ("I'm in a bind" v.22); and then screams either in fear of rape or in search of help. The prayer she addresses to God is now in response to the guilty verdict rather than to the entrapment by the elders; and while continuing to affirm God's knowledge of the truth, the tale now includes a tortured inquiry - "Must I now die?" - that reflects her pious resignation to divine will.

The inner characters of the elders similarly expand, this time in the direction of villainy. They spy on the young woman day after day. No longer disassociated from her person, Susanna's beauty triggers a lust and a passion that they are embarrassed to admit even to each other; their attempt to "force her" not only is premeditated (v.14), but dialogically developed (v. 20); and their perjured account of the encounter involves not simply sight of the fictitious young lover, but an effort to capture him that is frustrated by his (youthful) physical strength (v. 39).

Daniel's part in the story also changes. No longer is he the vehicle for the workings of a divinely appointed angel in pursuit of justice. The holy spirit working within him, Daniel draws the crowd's attention with a personal protest against the guilty verdict - "I am innocent of this woman's blood" - and then

---

[8] The earliest date claimed for the revised version is the middle of the first century B.C.E. See Emanuel Tov, *Textual Criticism of the Hebrew Bible* (Philadelphia: Fortress Press, 1992).

proceeds to interrogate the perjurers. That scene is similar to the Old Greek one; but it has a totally new ending that both fleshes out the focus on characters and alters the moral point of the tale. The crowd and, until now, silent parents and husband glorify God "who saves those who trust in him;" and Daniel gains great reputation in the eyes of the people.[9]

The revised story was attributed to Theodotion who lived at the end of the second century C.E. and who was described by Irenaeus as a Jewish proselyte and by Jerome as a "heretic and judaizer."[10]   However, since citations from the so-called Theodotion text appear in sources predating the translator's time, the early history of this later narrative is also not clear.[11] Both versions were known in the early Christian period, but sometime in the third century C.E. the Theodotion text totally displaced the Old Greek one. We have little knowledge of the processes involved in that displacement.[12] Yet it is noteworthy that the areas where the Theodotion most radically departs from the Old Greek - the elevation of heroic and villainous characterization over communal, legal issues and the absence of explicit, positive Jewish associations (i.e., no reference to Susanna as "Jewess" and the synagogue no longer the scene of justice)[13] - are particularly significant when the story becomes intertwined with the development of Christian self definition.

The interest of the Church Fathers in *Susanna* arose in the context of the

---

[9] However, even in this ending no attention is given to Susanna as a character. For a reading of the story as a "construct of the relationship between gender and ethnicity," see A. J. Levine, "'Hemmed In On Every Side:' Jews and Women in the Book of Susanna," in *Reading From This Place*, S. Segovia and M. Tolbert, eds. (Fortress Press: Philadelphia, 1994).

[10] Irenaeus, *Against Heresies* 21.1 and Jerome, *Apology* 2.33. Suzanne Daniel suggests that much as Aquila and the targumist Onkelos may be the same person, so the name Theodotion "recalls that of the targumist Jonathan" ("The Bible: Translations - Greek", *Encyclopedia Judaica* [Jerusalem: Keter Publishing House, 1972] IV, 855).

[11] Developing the theory of an earlier, proto-Theodotion, translation upon which the Theodotion version was based, some scholars argued that it, like the earlier version, was based on a Semitic *Vorlage*. Others however maintained that the Daniel text attributed to Theodotion is an editorial revision of the Old Greek story without reference to a Semitic base. Most recently, the argument for a proto-Theodotion has been replaced by that of the *Kaige* Theodotion text with the presumed date of the middle of the first century B.C.E. On the complex problem of origins, see Moore, 30ff., 81ff. and Frank Zimmerman, "The Story of Susanna and Its Original Language," *JQR* 48 (1957-59), 236-41, P. Grelot, "Les versions grecques de Daniel." *Biblica* 47 [1966], 381-402, L. Hartman and A. A. Di Lella, *The Book of Daniel* (Anchor Bible 23; Garden City, NY: Doubleday, 1978), 76-84, and most recently, Tov.

[12] Both versions were available to Origen in the first half of the third century, but he focussed on the Theodotion version. See the Prologue and comments on 13.8 in Jerome's *Commentary on Daniel*. Jerome also notes that the churches publicly read Daniel in accord with the Theodotion, rather than the Old Greek text (Prologue, *Commentary on Daniel*.)

[13] For a detailed examination of the thematic changes, see Robert Doran, "The Additions to Daniel," *Harpers Bible Commentary* (San Francisco: Harper and Row, 1988), 864-866.

evolution of the Christian canon and the attempt on the part of early Christianity to come to grips with its Jewish past. That past was particularly troublesome to the early Church. On the one hand, Jewish roots provided continuity and highly valued evidence of antiquity for the new faith. On the other, any evidence of the vitality or persistence of the "Old Israel" involved a de facto threat to the claims of continuity and replacement by the "New." Consequently, walking a thin line, the Church strove to authenticate its link to the Jews (in the positive context called "the Hebrews") and at the same time to discredit them (in the negative context, called "the Jews"). The Fathers employed *Susanna* to work both sides of the precarious endeavor. The context of her labor was twofold: historical authentication of the Christian canon and exegetical support for the development of Christian theology and doctrine. In the writings of the Church Fathers the two areas are intertwined; but for purposes of clarity, I will momentarily separate them.

The canonical issue is initially addressed by Hippolytus of Rome (170?-235), the first known Christian exegete to focus extensively on the Susanna story. He begins by placing Susanna within a context dear to the Church Fathers - the tradition of Hebrew prophets. Her father, Hippolytus informs us, was "Chelcias the priest who found the book of law," and the father of the prophet Jeremiah (vs. 1) - and thus Susanna was the prophet's sister. Far more interested in exegesis than in canonical issues, Hippolytus still had to deal with the fact that the Susanna narrative was not found in the book of Daniel in Hebrew Scriptures. He accounts for its problematic absence with the charge that "the rulers of the Jews (the rabbis?) wish now to expunge those things from the book and assert the things did not happen in Babylon because they were ashamed of what was done then by the elders" (Commentary, "On Susanna" v. 8). There is a kind of perversity to his elevation of Susanna's lineage and a gratuitous quality to his charge against the "Jewish rulers" for as we shall see when we turn to Hippolytus's exegesis, the true meaning of the story is an embedded allegorical one and the events "happened at a later time" than the position of the narrative at the beginning of the book of Daniel would indicate (Preface, Commentary, "On Susanna").[14]

His claim that the leaders of the Jews had purposely tampered with the text of Daniel in order to hide evidence of their calumnies anticipates a more intensive attack on the story just a bit later by Africanus, a Christian, but non-clerical, scholar. Arguing from the style as well as the substance of the story, Africanus labelled *Susanna* a spurious, "modern forgery." His critique is multifaceted. The story is not consistent with the book of Daniel for instead of visions and dreams, the prophet here is moved by divine inspiration. The puns work in Greek, but not in Hebrew and hence could not have been part of a Hebrew original. More historically, he questions how a people who supposedly

---

[14] In the Old Greek the Susanna addition is placed after Daniel 12, whereas in the Theodotion version it comes at the beginning of Daniel.

are exiles living in captivity could possess such wealth and independence in judicial matters. The heart of his objections, however, is the known fact that "this section, along with the other two at the end of it, is not contained in the Daniel received among the Jews" ("A Letter to Origen from Africanus About the History of Susanna"). Origen (185-254), the Church Father to whom the questions were addressed, responds to all these points, but most revealingly to the issue of the Jewish canon. Using information he claimed to have acquired from his personal contacts with Jews, he argues that they did indeed know of the story. He tells Africanus that "a learned Hebrew said among them to be the son of a wise man and trained to succeed his fathers" had told him the names of the elders as they appeared in Jeremiah.[15] Moreover, another "Hebrew" had told him other stories about these elders, specifically, that they "deceived the wives of their countrymen" and "pretended to the Jews in captivity, who were hoping by the coming of Christ to be freed from the yoke of their enemies, that they could explain clearly the things concerning Christ."[16]

As for how the Susanna story came to be lost from the book of Daniel in Hebrew Scriptures, Origen's answer is substantively that of Hippolytus, but notably more vituperative in tone. Citing the tradition of the killing of the prophets as historical facts deleted from Hebrew Scriptures, Origen claims that "they (the leaders) hid from the knowledge of the people as many of the passages which contained any scandal against the elders, rulers, judges, as they could, some of which have been preserved in uncanonical writings." Moreover, "it would be nothing wonderful if this history were true, and the licentious and cruel attack was actually made on Susanna by those who were at that time elders, and written down by the wisdom of the Spirit, but removed by these rulers of Sodom as the Spirit would call them" ("A Letter from Origen to Africanus").

Origen's response reflects the problem the third century Church had with Judaism. On the one hand, the Jewish canon, albeit in need of reinterpretation, provided respectable antiquity and grounding for the new tradition. On the other, insofar as the sacred literature of the new tradition departed from that grounding, it could be called into question. Never a purely academic question,

---

[15] The reference is to the false prophets, Zedekiah and Ahab, mentioned in Jeremiah 29:22,23. On Origen's identification of the elders, see Jerome, *Commentary on Daniel* 13.1,2,5.

[16] Most likely this is a Christianized version of the rabbinic legend that has the false prophets of Jeremiah 29 entice women into sexual relations by telling them that God had commanded it. See Louis Ginzberg, *The Legends of the Jews* (Philadelphia: Jewish Publication Society, 1967) VI, 415.

His acquaintanceship with Jews aside, Origen's knowledge of biblical Hebrew is highly suspect. In an attempt to prove to Africanus that Greek translators could build a pun on a word derived from the same root which either corresponded to Hebrew or was analogous to it, he cites (אשא) from (כוס ישועות אשא) as the source for (אישה) - "taken from man." ("A Letter to Origen from Africanus About the History of Susanna").

the canonical issue was closely linked to the Church's theological need to identify itself over against Judaism. Both Hippolytus and Origen frame their "over against" as a confrontation with Jewish leadership. Unlike the Jewish masses, these leaders do not reject truth out of simple ignorance. To the contrary, they are malevolent deceivers. As Origen's version of the talmudic legend of the false prophets indicates, already in Babylonian captivity the Jewish people not only were aware of the significance of Christ, but also were anticipating His coming ("were hoping by the coming of Christ to be freed from the yoke of their enemies"). By all rights that anticipation should have prepared the way for the descendants of the captives to readily embrace the "good news" in the first century C.E. The fact that the Jews resisted the embrace, not only in the face of Christ but even continuing through to Origen's and Hippolytus's own era, required an explanation. The charge that Jewish leaders misled the people and then purposely distorted Scriptures in order to hide their own perversities provided just such an explanation. Although it sufficed to a degree theologically, it did not mark an end to questions about the authenticity of the Susanna addition to Daniel. That issue was raised again in the third century by the anti-Christian critic Porphry and yet a third time in an exchange between Rufinus and Jerome in the late fourth.

Before turning to the later period, however, we will look at how Susanna was treated in the development of ante-Nicean exegesis. Adopting Hebrew Scriptures as its own Old Testament, the Church had to reinterpret the text in a manner that would demonstrate both the rejection of Israel and its own claim to have replaced it. Such interpretations of Jewish texts were effected through the development of certain techniques that became the standard Christian mode of exegesis until challenged by the Northern humanists and the Reformers of the fifteenth and sixteenth centuries. The traditional Christian exegetical technique assumed that the true (spiritual) meaning of the Old Testament was a hidden one, buried in literal contexts. In order to unearth it, the exegete had to take the passage out of historical context, view it as a prefiguration of the New Covenant that would be established through Christ, and then develop an allegorical interpretation that could be applied typologically.

The references to Susanna in the writings of the Church Fathers of the second and early third centuries demonstrate various stages in the evolution of the method. Arguing that the true exposition of Scriptures is solely that of those who "possess the succession from the apostles" (i.e., those deemed authorities by the Church), Irenaeus, bishop of Lyons during the last quarter of the second century, describes presbyters (priests) of dissenting opinion as those who "serve their own lusts, and do not place the fear of God supreme in their hearts" and applies to them the words Daniel spoke against the perjuring elders (*Against Heresies* 26:3). Clearly there is no question of lust involved in the case of the opponents he is attacking there. Given the context of the work, the targets are most probably priests whose interpretations partake of a Gnostic character. But described as "presbyters," they are obviously people of some authority (and perhaps of some seniority) in the early Church community. Consequently, the attack requires a textual situation which demonstrates condemnation of established figures who have community respect, but who in fact mislead and distort truth. Such a model is found in the elders; and when the verses applied to them are displaced into a contemporary setting, their lust accompanies the move through time.

A different approach is taken by Clement (?-215) of Alexandria. An early adherent of the tradition that would combine Platonism with Christian doctrine, this Father points to the person of Susanna as evidence of the capacity of women to achieve Perfection. Paired with Miriam who is described as an "associate" of her brother (i.e., Jeremiah) and "superior to all women among the Hebrews who were in repute for their wisdom," Susanna achieves her Perfection as "the unwavering martyr of chastity" (*Stromata* iv.19). There is no displacement here. But Clement's treatment - Susanna as a model of chastity - involves its own distortion for in the context of the story the issue for Susanna is not the dearness of her own chastity, but the violation of God's Law. Nonetheless, in Christian exegesis the association between Susanna and the virtue of Chastity becomes a particularly close one. Irenaeus and Clement refer neither to Jews nor to Judaism in their comments on the character of Susanna. Yet Irenaeus's identification of his errant opponents with the lustful elders and Clement's substitution of chastity for fidelity to the Law as Susanna's chief concern suggest some associative imaging of Judaism, the elder religious tradition, as still erroneously holding to the covenantal vitality of the Law.

There is no such ambiguity in Hippolytus's reading. He develops a full allegorical treatment of the story that explicitly identifies at least one of the villainous elders with the Jews and blatantly deprives the heroic Susanna of her Jewish identification. The beautiful, pious woman "instructed in the Law of Moses" and wed to a powerful, but barely visible, aristocrat is transformed by allegory into the young Church wed to the power of Christ. Assuming new significance, Babylon becomes the unsafe "world" and the isolated garden where the Theodotion version of the tale is enacted, the home of the "saints who are planted fruitful trees in the Church" (v. 7).[17] In this Eden-like setting, on an Easter Sunday[18] the handmaids - Faith and Charity - prepare oil, representative of the power of the Holy Spirit, for the bath, symbol of baptism, of the young, vulnerable Church (v. 18). No longer villainous elders wounded by lust and seeking the destruction of the object of their rejected suit, the elders are two peoples - "the people of the circumcision" and the Gentiles - who, wounded by Satan, join forces (albeit temporarily) in their shared purpose to corrupt, bear false witness against, and destroy the Church (v. 10). In other words, spiritually and properly understood, the Jewish tale of Babylon is a

---

[17] Clearly the synagogue in which the judicial scene is housed in the Old Greek version would not be appropriate for this interpretation.
[18] He interprets the date from "they were watching closely for the opportune day" (v. 15).

prefigurement of the situation of the Church in Hippolytus's own day. No longer a Jewish sect and not yet adopted by pagan, imperial Rome, the fledgling Church that strives to maintain faith with her spouse, is, like Susanna, "straightened on every side" (v. 21). For Hippolytus, the Jewish alliance with Satan has deep roots, roots signalled by the parallel between Daniel's words - "I am innocent of the blood of this woman" (v. 46) - and those of Pilate - "I am innocent of the blood of this just person" (Matthew 27:24). Even before the Church became the vicar of Christ, the Jews conspired against Jesus, condemned him to death, and then attempted to heighten his pain by giving him vinegar and gall to drink in the hours of his suffering. For this they were humbled and made miserable.[19] The destruction of the elders through Daniel's prophetic gift foretells (prefigures) a comparable punishment for their heirs who persist in rejection and so, by their very existence, endanger the Church.

Like the Church that adopts her as its own alter ego, Susanna's Jewish roots are subsumed within a new persona. Dejudaized, she becomes an active participant in the development of Christian theology. The doctrine of original sin, the sacrificial character of clerical administration of the Lord's Supper, the notion that salvation is available exclusively through the Church ("catholic Christianity") as well as trinitarian Christology - were all being worked through in third century Christian controversy. None of these issues particularly involved Jews and/or Judaism. But insofar as the Jewish world was viewed as the old way, as a "past" fulfilled, and as legitimate only in present Christian form, it provided an antithetical model for Christian self definition. The dichotomies offered in the Theodotion version of the Susanna tale made it a particularly appealing structure within which to house such a model.

If Hippolytus makes Susanna the Church standing over against its external enemies, others use her to argue internal matters of Church policy and doctrine. Tertullian (155?-240), for example, attributes a guilt-ridden responsibility to Susanna, and cites her veiled state against those who would require women by law to cover their heads: "...the veil was a voluntary thing. She had come accused, ashamed of the disgrace she had brought on herself, properly concealing her beauty, even because now she feared to please" (The Chaplet). And Cyprian (200?-258), echoing Irenaeus, but better armed with the spiritual, allegorical, interpretation of the story at hand, charges his opponents with "re-echoing the old evil of the two elders" by attempting to corrupt the "chastity of the Church" with adulterated doctrines (Letters 43).

Gradually Susanna's person undergoes yet another change. Increasingly identified with Church, with purity and chastity, by the end of the century the wedded state so significant to the plot of her tale is ignored and she comes to be viewed as the embodiment of a maryological virginity (Methodius, "Banquet

---

[19] *Adversus Judaeos*, ch. 1. In fact the giving of vinegar and gall was intended to dull the pain. But the malevolent intent attributed to it by Hippolytus became the standard interpretation.

of the Ten Virgins"). The shift is a significant one; whereas Susanna was the newly dejudaized, endangered Church for the ante-Nicean Fathers, she enters the service of the imperial Church and post Nicean Fathers as the representation of a firm and steady Church. The vulnerable young wife ashamed of her own beauty becomes the new Eve, the strong, primal mother of all. Evident, but theologically underdeveloped in Hippolytus's exegesis of the garden scene, the transformation is assumed in the homiletical writings of Ambrose (337?-397) (*Three Books on the Duties of the Clergy*, I.18), Chrysostom (345?-407) ("On Susanna"), and of St. Asterius, the fourth century bishop of Amasus (*Sixth Homily*). Susanna's garden story is a return, a second chance so to speak, to Eden. This time, in deliberate and striking contrast to her primal counterpart, the new mother resists the tempting of Satan's agents; and consequently, like the Church that she prefigures, reverses the consequences of the fateful first Fall.[20] As for the elders, in the context of the new perspective, they cease to represent misguiding Jewish leadership and become either "the damned, alien to life and the workmen of sin" (St. Asterius, *Sixth Homily*) or all the Jews, the totally "other" who should be "passed by" as justly condemned by God for their malevolence (Gregory of Nazianzus [329?-389], *In Defense of His Flight to Pontus* and Sulpicius Severus [?-400?], Sacred History, II, Par. 1).

Oddly enough, Susanna's full entry into the theological world of the imperial Church did not mean the end of controversy over the canonical authenticity of her story. Writing a preface to the book of Daniel around the end of the fourth century, Jerome reopened that old issue by noting that the version read by the Church (the Theodotion text) was not the same as the Old Greek story and that the Hebrew Bible contained neither *Susanna* nor any of the other "Additions." Moreover, he had heard a certain Jewish teacher make objections comparable to those of Africanus and mock the "History of Susanna" as the "fiction of some Greek." The issue may have been a matter of scholarship for Jerome; but for his colleague and correspondent, Rufinus, it was one of great theological import - particularly with reference to the Jews. Expressing horror that Jerome should expose himself to a Jewish teacher - (Jerome had mentioned studying Aramaic ["Chaldee"] with a certain Jew) - Rufinus charges Jerome with "drawing from the 'Synagogue of Satan,'" i.e., with judaizing. As if the historical, contemporary context of the charge were insufficiently serious, Rufinus then goes on to place it in a scriptural context that suggests a kind of exegetical "postfigurement," i.e., prefigurement in reverse gear. Deliberately, if not maliciously, distorting the tutor's name from Baranina to Barabbas, he associates Jerome with the crowd of Jews who

---

[20] On the development of Susanna as Eve in Christian art, see M. C. Leach, "Rubens' *Susanna and the Elders* in Munich and Some Early Copies," in *Print Review* 5 (1976), 120-27 and Mary D. Garrard, "Artemisia and Susanna" in *Feminism and Art History: Questioning the Litany*, N. Braude and M. D. Garrard, eds. (New York: Harper and Row, 1982), 147-71.

favored release of a common criminal over Jesus (John 18:40). "From...Barabbas, whom you chose out of the synagogue rather than Christ, you learned to hope for a resurrection not in power but in frailty, to love the letter which kills and hate the spirit which gives life, and other more secret thing, which, if occasion so require, shall afterwards in due time be brought to life" (*Apology of Rufinus*, I.12).

No longer an issue of the authenticity and legitimacy of the Christian Old Testament, the controversy assumes the coloring of the debate over humanism/scholasticism in the sixteenth century "Reuchlin Affair" that it foreshadows. Like those scholastics, Rufinus turns a scholarly matter into a contest between Christendom and the Jews. It involves not only the ancient Jews who dared "to tamper with the records of the Church which have been handed down from the apostles," but also the contemporary ones who are "hurrying" Jerome "into this abyss of evil" (*Apology of Rufinus*, II.33). Retorting that he was simply describing, not legitimating, what Jews think about Scriptures, Jerome, in his turn, fore-echoes the "liberal" humanists who will defend ancient Jewish books by attacking Jews:[21] "Still I wonder that a man should read the version of Theodotion, the heretic and judaizer, and should scorn that of a Christian, simple and sinful though he may be" (*Jerome's Apology for Himself Against the Books of Rufinus*, II.33). Nonetheless, it is the Theodotion version of Susanna that is invited into the Latin Vulgate.

There is a sequel to the story of Susanna's journey among the Fathers, one which gives that story a peculiar twist. Employed through the centuries as a proof text against Jews and Judaism, *Susanna and the Elders* reappears in a Jewish form as part of a hostile derision of early Christian origins. Like the earlier one, the tale is an "addition," in this case, an interpolation by the hand of a Hebrew scribe into *Sefer Yosippon*, the tenth century Hebrew chronicle that was wrongly, but widely, attributed to the first century historian Josephus.[22]

---

[21] Attacking the Dominican effort to suppress the Talmud, humanists of the stature of Ulrich von Hutten, Johann Reuchlin, and even Erasmus of Rotterdam focussed on the Jewish background of the Dominican convert, Johannes Pfefferkorn: "The baptized Jew Pfefforkorn...gaily abandoned himself to a perfidious revenge, according to the traditional manner of his ancestors the Jews" (Johann Reuchlin, *Der Augenspiegel*, fol. 32b). "His parents are Jews, and he remains such even if he has plunged his unworthy body into the baptism of Christ" (Ulrich von Hutten, *Letters of Obscure Men*). "Pfefforkorn is revealed to be a true Jew...He appears quite typical of his race. His ancestors attacked Christ only, whereas he has attacked many worthy and eminent men. He could render no better service to his coreligionists than by betraying Christendom, hypocritically claiming to have become a Christian...This half-Jew has done more harm to Christendom than all the Jews together" (Letter from Erasmus to Pirkheimer, November 2, 1517; Letter to Reuchlin, November 15, 1517 in L. Geiger, *Johannes Reuchlin* [Leipzig, 1870]).

[22] See David Flusser, *The Josippon* (Jerusalem: Mosad Bialik, 1978-80) 2 vols. (Hebrew), Flusser, "The Author of Sefer Yosippon, His Character and Period," *Zion* 18 (1953) 109-26 (Hebrew); Israel Levi, "L'Histoire de 'Suzanne et les deux vieillards' dans la littérature juive," *Revue des Etudes Juives* 95 (1933), 157-71; Yitzhak Baer, "The Book of

This time the story takes place, not in an exilic situation, but in Judea in the first century C.E. Susanna is now named Chana. Wife of Channael the priest and daughter of Elyakim, High Priest from the Hasmonean line and a refugee from the persecutions of Herod, she still is pious and beautiful, indeed so much so that she is compared to Herod the Great's own Miriamne (Addition II, *Sefer Josippon*, 3-4). The setting for the infamous encounter is the garden of the estate of Chana's father, the High Priest to whom Judean elders and officials come for adjudication (6-7). Her husband having been sent by the king as part of a delegation to Rome, she stays with her father, piously going each day into the garden to pray for the well being of her spouse. Three (rather than two) of the many elders who frequent the house for judgment become enraptured by her beauty, devise their plot, and await the opportune time (7-9). When it comes, one of them grabs her, attempts to seduce her, and when twice refused threatens to charge her with adultery. No longer the shocked, hesitant Susanna of the Theodotion tale, she smartly answers: "We have learned that no ones dies on the word of one witness!" (10-13). In response, her attacker turns to his two comrades in seduction who assure her that they too will join in the charge and that as a daughter of a priest, she will be burned (13-15). Chana cries out as do her attempted seducers; the officials and elders come from the house; the perjured tale of the young lover "who got away" is told, but this time the woman is immediately judged and sentenced to death by burning (16-24). Here, instead of weeping on her behalf (*Susanna* v. 33), her female friends and companions accept her guilt, vilify and scorn her, and only her father, sure of her innocence, weeps on her behalf (24-25). As she comes past the Temple on route to execution of the sentence, she cries out her case before God (here citing Ezek 18:4, 20) (27-32). The divine response does not involve a young Daniel, but the spirit of a certain wise man named Nahman as well as that of the king who insists on a rehearing. With the puns omitted and the focus shifted to the absence of any of the three trees said by the perjurers to be in the garden, Nahman proves her innocence and the king orders her release (33-48). The villains are hung and Chana's name becomes a byword in blessing and prayer - "May God judge you as he judged between Chana and the perjurers" (49). The story is built off the Theodotion text,[23] and yet shows a concern

---

Josippon the Jew," in *Sefer Benzion Dinaburg*, Yitzhak Baer et al.,eds. (Jerusalem, 1949), 178-205; and Abraham Neuman, "Josippon and the Apocrypha," *JQR* 43 (1952-53), 1-26.

The interpolations appear in full in two manuscripts - the Rothshild (Oxford) and Kaufmann (Budapest) - dated before ibn Daud (1160). In later versions they are abbreviated and/or deleted by the censor. That the addition duplicates notice of Gaius's death in a subsequent chapter of the original *Josippon* indicates that its purpose was not to supplement *Josippon*. Rather, it was written independently and later inserted into the text. For the text of the interpolation, see Flusser, *The Josippon*, II, 442-44.

[23] Note the following parallels in detail: the threat of the elders Jos.10/Susanna 21; the perjured account of the attempt to capture the young man Jos.19/Susanna 39; God's knowledge of her innocence Jos.30/Susanna 43; praise of God at the end Jos.48/Susanna

with matters of justice that recalls the old Greek version. More important from our perspective, the text and context of this narrative suggest that its author not only was aware of the exegetical tradition of the Church Fathers, but also deliberately constructed his own tale in response to that tradition.

The tale presents positive characterizations of the institutions of Second Temple Judaism that are most disparaged in Christian tradition. The high quality of Chana's family credentials rests not on a prophetic connection, but on a priestly one. Not only is her husband a member of the priestly clan, but her father is the High Priest; and when all others succumb to belief in the perjured testimony, he alone retains faith in his daughter's innocence. Moreover, the High Priest's home is the place where the elders of Judea seek justice; and when that system falls into error, it is at the Temple that Chana's call for divine assistance is heard. The response is no miraculous insight on the part of a young boy, but a new trial called by the king where through the talents of a wise man learned in the art of interrogation the earlier judicial wrong is redressed.[24]

The context of the medieval recast tale is even more telling. It is immediately preceded by another interpolation inserted into Josippon's narrative of the Roman Emperor Gaius Caligula (chapter 49 after line 15). This interpolation involves another trial and the beginning of Christianity.[25] The narrative describes Jesus and two disciples going to Emperor Gaius Caligula with the claim that God had sent Jesus to anoint Gaius and to establish worship of him as a god. The three complain that when they had attempted to convey this revelation to their own people, the Jews had rejected it and sought to kill them. Consequently, Gaius sends his statue to Jerusalem with the command that he be worshipped (Addition I, *Sefer Josippon*, 10-18). The Judeans refuse it entry, and send their own delegation to the Roman emperor to explain that the Nazarene and his followers are Jewish apostates who speak untruth and misinterpret the Torah. In fury Gaius ejects the delegation and the Jewish nation turns in fasting and prayer to God (21-39). The response is not long to come. Conspirators kill the Emperor (while he seeks enjoyment at the Hippodrome no less); the just Claudius replaces him and turns Jesus and the other traitors over to the Jerusalem authorities (40-48). They are tried by the law of the king before the Sanhedrin, and in accord with that law are found guilty and hung. In the belief that the crime was a product of Judean factionalism and that the guilty three would in fact repent and "return," some opposed the extreme sentence. But the majority supported the authorities because the dissenters had tried to incite Rome to war against the nation

---

62-63.

[24] Attention is also paid to halakhic detail, e.g., Chana is made the daughter of a priest and sentenced to death by burning. The three, instead of two, "witnesses" may reflect the discussion of *Sota* 31b.

[25] The interpolation is found in Flusser, *The Josippon*, v. I, 439-442.

(49-55). However, in spite of the execution, many secretly continued to follow the Nazarenes and their evil teachings became widespread (56-59).

Most probably the author of this tale of Christian origins is the same person who developed the Chana tale that immediately follows it.[26] With minimal interpretation, it could be argued that the author/interpolator introduced the Chana story specifically after the Jesus story in order to demonstrate the high quality of Judean justice under the king's law. There are a number of obvious parallels between the two stories. Both involve justice, trials and a matter of adjudication; both have three "perjurers;" both attribute the victory of justice to divine intervention; and both celebrate the law of the king.

But employing a broader interpretive brush, one might also argue that the two interpolations should be treated as a single unit in which the two texts interplay as text and subtext. Such an interpretation clarifies how the story of Susanna became the tale of Chana. The medieval Jewish author adopts Susanna as she came to be in allegorical service of the Church. Susanna, the Church, returns as Chana, the Synagogue. The three who attempted to entrap Chana into adultery are the same as Jesus and his disciples who attempted to entrap the Jews into idolatry. Their apostasy, like the community's initial compliance with the elders, might be innocently attributable to blindness by reason of circumstance - much as the Church at first viewed the Jewish error. To the wise like Nahman and the rabbis of the Sanhedrin, however, the malevolent intent is always clear. And as the apostates increase in power and number, the enlightened community comes to realize that only God's intervention can stop them. Thus, the author of the interpolations brings Susanna into yet another context. The paired interpolations suggest he does so in full awareness of the nature of her service with the Church Fathers. For the malevolence attributed to the Jews in the course of the tale's journey in Christendom - misrepresentation and distortion of Scriptures - is here turned back on the founders of Christianity: "They spoke things of the Lord Our God which we do not teach and they altered the meaning of the Torah" (28-29).

---

[26] Flusser, *The Jossipon*, Introductory note, 442.

Susanna as Parable: A Response to Piero Boitani

Harold Fisch
Bar-Ilan University

In addition to giving us a fascinating glimpse of Roman life (and death) in the first Christian centuries, Professor Boitani has shown the remarkable centrality of the Susanna story for the early Church. It evidently supplied one of the six or seven most important scenes from the Old Testament to be found in Christian iconography, especially as displayed in funerary art and inscriptions. Susanna and the Elders ranks, it seems, with Adam and Eve, the story of Noah and his ark, the sacrifice of Isaac and the scene of Moses striking the rock. In comparison, from the Jewish side where the story of Susanna undoubtedly originated, there is total silence. No trace of the original Hebrew text has survived, and there are no references to the story in any classical rabbinic source. The versions which turn up in Adolf Jellinek's collection[1] and that of Moses Gaster[2] are late re-translations from the Greek of Theodotion.[3]

I want to speculate briefly on this silence and then say something about the possible reasons for the peculiar interest the text had for the early Church. First, the truth is that books that didn't get into the Hebrew canon tended to be ignored and nearly all of them have survived only in translations; in this respect Susanna is not unique. The real question is not why the silence, but why a particular text did not make it into the canon. In the case of Susanna, I think we may rule out the notion of Hippolytus[4] that "the chiefs of the Jews" proscribed the book "because they were ashamed of what their elders did at that time"--a view echoed by Origen in the same period. If two corrupt elders tried

---

[1] Adolf Jellinek ed., *Beth-Hamidrash* [Hebrew], vol 6 (1878; 2nd ed. Jerusalem: Bamberger and Wahrmann 1938), 126-128.

[2] Moses Gaster ed., *The Chronicles of Jerahmeel*, Oriental Translation Fund, NS vol. 4 (1899), 200-205.

[3] For further details see Yonah Cohen, s.v. "Ma'se shoshanna" in *Encyclopedia of Narrative Themes in the Literature of the Jewish People* [in Hebrew], ed. Yoav Elstein, in preparation.

[4] Cited by Boitani--see above p. 13.

to seduce Susanna, whom they found bathing, and then having failed in their attempt, brought a false charge of adultery against her, the canonical books of the Old Testament preserve reports no less scandalous about the sons of Eli the High Priest (I Samuel 2:22-26). Moreover, when Samuel, Eli's successor, became old in his turn, his sons, who were judges in Beer-Sheba, were, it seems not much better (ibid., 8:1-2). There is no attempt at a cover-up. And of course there is the affair of King David and Bathsheba (II Samuel 11:2-15). Whilst some of the talmudic Rabbis tried to explain away this ignominious episode,[5] there is again no attempt to suppress or censor the record itself. The prophet Jeremiah likewise names two false prophets, Zedekiah and Ahab, who specialized in seducing their neighbor's wives and ended up by being roasted in the fire by the King of Babylon! (Jeremiah 29:22-23). According to the elaboration of this mini-narrative in the Talmud, these two questionable characters over-reached themselves by turning their attentions to the daughter of Nebuchadnezzar himself![6] This story by the way, like the tale of Susanna, is located in Babylon at the time of Daniel and his friends, Hananiah, Mishael and Azariah. Origen claims to have it from a Jewish informant that these two false prophets named by Jeremiah were in fact the same two "ancient judges" referred to in the Tale of Susanna![7]

Be that as it may, from these analogous instances, we can safely dismiss the conspiracy theories of Origen and Hippolytus. If Susanna didn't make it into the canon, it was not because the story exposed the misdoings of the corrupt elders. Why then was the story not admitted? I will suggest two reasons. One is--to put it simply--that literary and dramatic qualities are not enough. The story proved attractive not only to the painters of the catacombs but also to modern writers from Shakespeare to James Bridie.[8] It has dramatic symmetry and power, a fine peripateia, and lots of human interest. But the Rabbis did not share the aesthetic standards of the Greeks and Romans. The Book of Esther offers us an even more powerful narrative, but we are told that Esther had great difficulty in persuading the Rabbis to admit her story into the canon! The Talmud pictures a little scene in which Esther begs the sages: "Put me into a book."[9] They are reluctant to do so and accept her story as holy writ only when they are persuaded that its importance and truth are vouched for in the Pentateuch itself.

In other words for a book to qualify, it has to serve purposes which go back to the beginnings of covenantal history, or Heilsgeschichte. By contrast,

---

[5] BT Shabbat, folio 56a, b.

[6] BT Sanhedrin, folio 93a.

[7] "Origen to Africanus" in *The Writings of Origen*, trans. F. Crombie, vol. I, in Ante-Nicene Christian Library, ed. A Roberts and J. Donaldson, vol X (Edinburgh: T.& T. Clark 1869), 376.

[8] See M. Roston, *Biblical Drama in England* (London: Faber 1968), 128, 282-283 and passim.

[9] BT Megilla, folio 7a.

Susanna is a domestic, moral tale lacking the epic, national overtones of Ruth or Esther. To use the term which I have used elsewhere to define the specific determinant of biblical poetics, I would want to say that a text must also be a testimony.[10] Esther, reflecting the existential crisis which besets the Jewish collectivity in the conditions of exile, is such a testimony; Susanna is not. Another reason, I suspect, why Susanna did not qualify is that it is at bottom more like a midrash--a kind of exegetical gloss--than an independent work in its own right. The text which it seems to gloss is the Song of Solomon.

Shoshana is of course the lily of that Song--*šošannat ha'amaqîm*.[11] And the use of the name takes us back inevitably to the Song of Solomon as the prime text for any discussion of Susanna:

> I am the tulip of the Sharon, the lily of the vallies.
> Like the lily among thorns, so is my love among the daughters.
> (Song 2:1-2)

The tale of Susanna would seem to be essentially a parable on the phrase "like the lily among thorns" (*kešošannâ bên haHohim*). The lily is traditionally understood in this context as representing the people of Israel--the thorns are the tribulations which Israel has endured over the centuries. Scores of existing midrashim make this point.[12] Interestingly, David Altschuler (18c) in his popular commentary "Metzudat David" uses the imagery of sexual solicitation to explain the meaning of "a lily among thorns": Even though the idol-worshippers seek to seduce you to go astray after them, you do not consent to them nor do you heed them. The author of Susanna is saying the same thing but building it up into a little story or parable, as midrash often does.

There are other details which inevitably recall the Song of Solomon. Chief among these is the setting of the enclosed garden. Susanna asks her maids to "shut the garden doors that I may wash me." The whole action of the story takes place in, or has reference to, the locked garden, the *hortus inclusus*. In the Song of Solomon the Shulammite herself had been identified with that garden: "a garden enclosed is my sister my bride" (4:12). But the garden was also the charmed space in which the whole action of the poem unfolded, a space threatened by "little foxes," by hostile watchmen, and by unkind brothers. Ambiguously, it was also the space in which the divine lover, the *dôd*, pastures his flocks among the lilies and seeks and finds his heart's desire. The garden of *Susanna and the Elders* has been seen in at least one medieval text as

---

[10] See H. Fisch, *Poetry With A Purpose: Biblical Poetics and Interpretation* (Bloomington: Indiana University Press 1988), 50-68.

[11] Lily (*lilium candidum*) has come to stay in the English versions, though the flower referred to is more probably a narcissus or a wild daffodil. Lotus has also been suggested but with less plausibility.

[12] See *Midrash Rabbah: Song of Songs*, trans. M. Simon, in *The Midrash*, vol. IX (London: Soncino Press 1939), 94-99.

converging with the symbolism of the enclosed garden of the Song of Solomon.[13] This convergence can also be traced in modern American romance as Sharon Baris has shown in her very suggestive essay on Hawthorne's story "Rappaccini's Daughter."[14] All this helps to explain the literary resonance of the Susanna story but it also serves to underline its possibly derivative character--a character common to many of the apocryphal writings.

Why then does the book come to be of such importance to the Church? One answer could be: for the same reason that it was less than supremely important for the Jewish sages. Parable is in the Jewish literary tradition the appropriate mode for midrash. For the Christian literary tradition, it is the essential mode of gospel, the heart of the Christian message being expressed in parable.[15] In parable or exemplum, I should add, moral clarity is matched by artistic balance. There are five foolish virgins and five wise virgins, the disappointment suffered by the former balancing exactly the success achieved by the latter. The prudent husbandman sows good seed, his enemy sows tares, but when the harvest comes the husbandman has his servants separate the tares from the wheat.

Old Testament narrative represents a more impure mode. The tares, we might say, are not so easily separated from the wheat. In the story of David, the noble and the ignoble, triumph and defeat, strength and weakness are less clearly and symmetrically marked off from one another. These more untidy narratives have the tang of lived history but they do not lend themselves so well to the neat contrasts and pairings which the painter of the frescoes in the catacombs of Priscilla achieved in his illustrations from Susanna. These have a pleasing economy of form and Professor Boitani does well to stress this quality. We might want to generalize and suggest that parable has a fundamentally synchronic character. Thus early and late balance one another symmetrically on either wall of the Greek chapel. Their diachrony is only an apparent diachrony. Even when the story is re-translated into new events, a process which Professor Boitani discusses at the end of his essay, those events seem not so much to be new as to be reenactments of an existing paradigm. Instead of an advance on an historical axis, with all the existential terror of the unexpected which this involves, we have the same "pleasing economy of form" constantly reconfirmed in a kind of ascending spiral.

But this does not wholly explain the popularity of the book and its importance for Christian theologians. As Professor Boitani has shown, Susanna rises to glory. She is not merely the heroine of an exemplary moral tale; she becomes a figure for the Church, her trial and near-execution prefiguring the

---

[13] See Alfred L. Kellogg, "Susannah and the Merchant's Tale," *Speculum* 35 (1960), 275.

[14] "Giovanni's Garden: Hawthorne's Hope for America," *MLS* (1982), 75-89.

[15] On the importance of the parable-form in the New Testament, see R.W. Funk, *Language, Hermeneutic and the Word of God* (New York: Harper and Row, 1968), 129, 212, etc.

trial and passion of Jesus himself with whom she shares the same messianic ancestry. One may argue that there is nothing new in this: Adam, says the apostle Paul in his Letter to the Romans, "is the figure of him that was to come" (5:14). And we recall the instruction in typology which the angel Michael gives to Adam in Paradise Lost, Book XII, showing him how the "shadowy types" of the Old Covenant are changed from flesh to spirit, from works of law to works of faith. His prime example, taken from the epistle to the Hebrews (cf. 4:8) is that of Joshua:

> And therefore shall not Moses, though of God
> Highly beloved, being but the minister
> Of law, his people into Canaan lead;
> But Joshua whom the gentiles Jesus call,
> His name and office bearing........(*Paradise Lost* XII.307-311)

To make Joshua, the military conqueror of Canaan, into a type of Christ (in the phrase "whom the gentiles Jesus call" we hear also the echo of "gentle Jesus") involves a radical revision and rethinking of an existing text. Typology is from this point of view essentially antithetical.[16] As Herbert Marks has noted, "the 'fulfilment' of the Old Testament text may be said to entail its simultaneous annulment"; what is involved is "a strong negative contrast between type and antitype."[17] This hermeneutical tension is clearly present in the re-reading of the figure of Joshua needed to make him into a type of Christ.

From this point of view "Susanna and the Elders" would seem to enjoy great advantages as a text for typological interpretation; for the tension involved in the "negative contrast between type and antitype" is here notably absent. The Rabbis had never appropriated the book and therefore when Susanna is seen as a figure of Jesus or the Church, there is no other case to be answered. At the same time the text comes with the commanding priority of its Hebrew origin. This is the main thrust of Origen's reply to Africanus; he argues for that priority. For if it is a Hebrew book, then it has the authority of "Hebrew truth." Paradoxically, that authority comes here to support the Christian reading, any competing interpretation having gone by default!

More than that, the Rabbis through their silence would be seen as tacitly concurring with the Christian reading. If the book manifestly speaks against the "ancient judges" viz., the scribes and the pharisees, condemning them as false witnesses, then we have here the silent testimony of those self-same pharisees to confirm this. There is a certain circularity, if not a contradiction, in all this, but it is easily overlooked in the excitement generated by the discovery of so many manifest affinities. For Origen we may suspect a felt affinity with the

---

[16] See Kenneth Gross, *Spenserian Poetics: Idolatry, Iconoclasm, and Magic* (Ithaca: Cornell University Press 1985), 60f.

[17] See Herbert Marks, "Pauline Theology and Revisionary Criticism," *Journal of the American Academy of Religion* vol. 52 (1984), 71-92. (Citations are from p. 78).

figure of Daniel who, according to one view at least, had also made himself a eunuch for the sake of the kingdom of heaven.[18] For Hippolytus the Church in Rome was manifestly threatened by the two false elders all over again, viz. by the Jewish and gentile communities of Rome. In such circumstances, the spokesmen of the Church were simply drawing attention to the reenactment of the Susanna story in their own time and place, with themselves performing the master-role of Daniel, the true judge who exposes the falsehoods of the circumcised and uncircumcised alike.

But the ultimate value of this text was that it was above all things an allegory of the hermeneutic process itself. The garden is the scene of interpretation. The elders are doing what the Jews have always done, viz., wrongly interpreting their own Scriptures, thus bearing false witness. In the action of the story they are silenced by Daniel, the man greatly beloved, who defeats them through the power, authority and insight which he brings to bear on the understanding of the same text. The garden is the scene of interpretation and what did or did not happen in the garden is the matter to be interpreted. The vindication of the righteousness of Susanna is the victory of true over false interpretation. The story thus enacts the victory of the Church over the Synagogue. The false elders seek to suppress the truth and replace it with their own falsehood. The marvelous outcome is however in the words of the story itself, that "Daniel convicted them of false witness out of their own mouth." For the story of their false witness is paradoxically the authentic record that they had themselves authored and one which the Church had preserved in spite of the authors' own attempts to suppress it!

The subtlest turn in this allegory of the hermeneutic process comes it would seem in Hippolytus's comment on verse 21 where the two elders tell Susanna that if she does not consent to yield to them "we will bear witness against thee, that a young man was with thee." Here Hippolytus springs a surprise, saying: And there was in reality a young man with her, that one of yours, one from heaven [meaning Daniel or perhaps Jesus], not to have intercourse with her, but to bear witness to her truth.[19] Here is what Harold Bloom would call a transumptive strategy whereby the late becomes early and the early becomes late.[20] Daniel, representing the Christian reading, is already in the garden when the false elders tell their false story. In other words, the interpreter places himself and his reading in a position of priority vis-à-vis the precursor-text, making the later precede the earlier. His true reading of the

---

[18] On Origen's alleged self-castration, see Eusebius, *Ecclesiastical History*, Book 6, section 8 in Loeb Classical Library edition, vol II, trans. J.E.L. Oulton (Cambridge Mass.: Harvard University Press 1932), 29-31. The case of Daniel is discussed in BT Sanhedrin, folio 93b.

[19] Hippolytus, *Fragments from his Commentaries*.....trans. S.D.F. Salmond, in *Ante-Nicene Christian Library*, ed. cit., vol VI, 480.

[20] See Harold Bloom, *A Map of Misreading* (New York: Oxford University Press 1975), 103, 130-131.

scene precedes their false reading. But by an irony which seems to have escaped Hippolytus, the presence of a "young man" who had secretly planted himself in the garden, is also the reinstatement in a work of Christian exegesis of that selfsame false testimony which the Jewish hero of the Jewish book of Susanna had successfully overthrown.

Sexuality and Social Control:
Anthropological Reflections on the Book of Susanna[1]

Susan Sered and Samuel Cooper
Bar-Ilan University

MORAL SUPERIORITY AND STRUCTURAL INFERIORITY

The story of Susanna is fundamentally a gendered story. The gender identities of the protagonist (Susanna), her champion (Daniel) and of the villains (the Elders) are crucial to the cultural message which the story conveys. The particular danger which threatens Susanna is a gendered danger (rape). Her pious reputation is framed in gendered terms (proper sexual behavior) as is the defamation of her character (accusation of adultery). Her initial punishment is a gendered punishment (publicly uncovering her face, as was done in the biblical ritual for determining if a woman had committed adultery). The motivation of the villains is a gendered motivation (heterosexual lust) and their tactic is a gendered tactic (sexual blackmail and threat of rape). In this paper we examine the cultural construction of gender in the Book of Susanna, in the context of a broad reading of gender in biblical and pseudepigraphic texts, structural analysis, and contemporary feminist theory.[2]

The Book of Susanna sets up a series of binary oppositions which are so strikingly detectable as to read almost like an essay by Claude Levi-Strauss.

Susanna	is to	The Elders	as
Female	is to	Male	as
Good	is to	Bad	as
Young	is to	Old	as
Powerless	is to	Powerful	as
Honest	is to	Dishonest	as
Beautiful	is to	Ugly (implicitly)	as

---

[1] Our comments in this paper draw upon the Theodotion version.

[2] We realize that there are other readings of this story. Within Jewish tradition, the Susanna story's chief salience has to do with legal requirements of witnesses.

Victorious	is to	Defeated as
Pious	is to	Hypocritical as
Inarticulate	is to	Articulate as
Solitary	is to	Group-oriented as
Private	is to	Public as
Chaste	is to	Sexual

Stories of good vs. evil, and the triumph of good over evil, are common cross-culturally. As Levi-Strauss (1963) argued, there seems to be some sort of elemental human appeal to "good guy vs. bad guy" stories. The question that interests us here is less the **universality** of these schemas than the **particularity**; that is, what particular traits are aligned with or opposed to each other in specific cultural contexts. Given the highly gendered nature of the Book of Susanna, we can treat the constellations of traits associated with Susanna or the Elders as cultural indicators of gender roles and expectations.

Femaleness, in this story, is aligned with a range of traits indicative of structural weakness; in fact, Susanna is attributed so many tokens of structural weakness that one suspects the author of wanting to ensure that the reader cannot possibly miss the message - Susanna has no access to socially recognized power. She is a female in a society in which the community leaders (including her husband) are male. She is young in a society in which being an "Elder" is a rank of community leadership. She is isolated and alone: no one in the community - including her own natal family - comes to her defense. She is inarticulate - she is either unwilling or unable to defend herself when accused. She is vulnerable to sexual attack. And, most of all, she is simple - she devises no plan to contest the Elders' sophisticated and intricate accusation. In summary, the traits associated with Susanna hammer in the message that women have no access to structural strength. Susanna's passivity is already previewed in the opening lines of the Book which begins not with Susanna herself, but with "There was a man living in Babylon whose name was Joakim. And he took a wife named Susanna."

At first reading, Susanna's wealth can cloud her weakness and camouflage her in an aura of structural superiority - her hundreds of relatives and servants seem to proclaim to the reader that here is a powerful person. However, a closer reading indicates the opposite: the wealth does not belong to Susanna but to her husband; she is surrounded by family and servants but no one affords her an opportunity to defend herself; and despite her high socio-economic class the town is quite willing to believe the worst of her. In other words, the story demonstrates that gender status and socio-economic status cross-cut one another; wealth does not ameliorate women's subordination. Susanna's ostentatious affluence serves to underscore the book's message - her material riches dramatize her structural poverty.

The Elders, as we can see, are presented as the mirror-image of Susanna; they are associated with a long list of "strong" characteristics. They are community leaders, articulate, knowledgeable about how things work in the public sphere, old, and, above all, male.

Yet our argument is not that Susanna has no strength. Our argument is that she has no **structural** strength. Although she has no access to public power or influence, she represents a form of **moral** strength which, in the end, defeats the structural strength of the Elders. Together with her structural weakness, Susanna's moral strength is introduced right at the beginning of the text; in 1:3 we read that she "feared the Lord. Her parents were righteous and had taught their daughter according to the law of Moses." Of what is Susanna's moral strength characterized in the course of the story? Susanna, through passivity and silence, epitomizes absolute faith in God. Returning to our lists of binary traits, we see that piety is associated with femaleness, simplicity, passivity, silence, honesty, and the private sphere. In contrast to the socially constructed public strength of the male Elders, Susanna epitomizes privately constructed moral strength which differs in every conceivable way from the public power of the Elders.

Our argument up to here can be summarized in this way. The Book of Susanna contrasts two types of strength: structural and moral. Structural strength is associated with maleness, and is presented as both inconsistent with moral strength, and inferior to it. Moral strength is associated with femaleness, and is presented as the antithesis of structural strength, and superior to it.

This analysis is quite consistent with sociological and anthropological literature on the "powers of the weak." Victor Turner (1974) and others have argued that in a variety of cultural situations structural weakness is associated with moral strength. The feminization of religion in nineteenth century American culture, which presupposed and reinforced women's exalted moral status and their secondary social status (Welter 1974), is one example of this phenomenon. The common, dramatic, and often pornographic portrayals of early Christian women martyrs as earning moral victories against their powerful, pagan male torturers further clarifies the association of structural weakness with moral strength and women (cf. Brock and Harvey 1987; Boitani, this volume.)

DANIEL, GENDER AND TRANSFORMATION

However, and this is where both our argument and the Book of Susanna become more complex, if the binary scheme which we have presented is "true," one would expect that Susanna's vindication would come about through unqualified divine intervention in order for the community to witness that Susanna's piety elicited divine reward. This kind of finale would clarify that Susanna was being honored for her moral superiority without muddying the stage with any shred of structural strength. Instead, Susanna's vindication comes about through a human source, Daniel, who is far more concerned with condemning the Elders than with championing Susanna. In fact, Susanna's piety is irrelevant to Daniel's legal machinations. Her moral strength is not really rewarded; rather, the Elders' behavior is condemned.

Returning to our lists of binary oppositions, Daniel introduces something of a predicament - he seems bent on confusing our binary scheme. We have presented a culture highly bifurcated in regard to gender, a culture in which a wide range of behavioral and attitudinal traits are associated with maleness or femaleness. Daniel, dropping in from outside the cultural boundaries of the town inhabited by Susanna and the Elders, obfuscates gender expectations: Daniel is associated with traits from both lists. In common with Susanna, Daniel is young, structurally powerless (he is not a public official), and pious. Like the Elders, he is male, sophisticated, and articulate. Yet somehow these mutually exclusive constellations seem to "work" in the person of Daniel. We argue that Daniel embodies a transformative role - he not only transforms Susanna from condemned to victorious and the Elders from powerful to denounced, but he also transforms traits of weakness to traits of strength. Daniel - like Batman or Robin - appears out of the blue, with no position or past, a young male similar in gender to the Elders, innocent and pure of motive like Susanna, and different from both Susanna and the Elders in that he has absolutely no background or status. He has neither the political status of the Elders nor the economic or moral status of Susanna; he has neither power nor wealth nor reputation.

Given Daniel's outsider status, it is crucial to ask why this young stranger was permitted to question the Elders. He had no structural power, he did not arrive with an army. Why, then, did the townspeople and Elders permit him to speak? In order to answer this question we momentarily step outside of the text, and point to the existence of numerous characters in primitive and folk societies who act similarly to Daniel (Dennis 1975; Cooper 1978). Most typically, these actors are social deviants, alien diviners, or children. These actors typically say things that need saying, yet that can only be said by someone who is too distant from important patterns of social relations to be affected by the matters at hand. The drunk, the crazed, or as in the case of Daniel - the young and the socially non-aligned individual, may serve society by saying and doing things which could not otherwise be said or done in public. The child or outsider can sometimes transmit messages which would normally remain unsaid simply because the saying violates some "higher" social order. The challenge to the Elders could not be made by anyone other than an innocent outsider, naive in the ways of society yet speaking the truth.

TRICKS AND GENDER

Within the biblical context - as in many other cultural contexts - the power of the weak often takes form through trickery and cunning. In biblical stories an extraordinarily large number of protagonists use trickery as a tool to attain their ends. **Many if not most of these trickster protagonists are female.** The claim to fame of biblical heroines is that they survive through their wits - trickery is their main, if not only, weapon (which is not surprising in patriarchal societies where women have no access to more direct means of power).[3] To take the most famous examples: Judith tricks Holifernes, the mother of the seven sons tricks the tyrant Antiochus, Rachel tricks everyone, Tamar tricks Judah, Rebecca tricks Isaac, Esther tricks Ahashueros, and we could go on and on. Despite the subordinate gender status of these protagonists and the questionable moral rectitude of lying and cheating, these tricks are typically interpreted in the text and in the Midrash as something essentially good and worthwhile.

Biblical women rarely represent a role of absolute opposition to men. Rather, as tricksters, they embody a transforming role. If males represent the rules of the system - the way in which social and moral categories are supposed to be, then females - tricksters - represent the ways in which social and moral categories can and must be manipulated for the ultimate good of the society. The classical biblical women protagonists engage in tricky transformations of situations which cannot otherwise be resolved within the framework of a rigid categorical system of rights and wrongs. Biblical women typically manipulate, weighing one value against another in order to work their way out of disastrous situations constructed by men. To take one example, Judith lies and kills because men have set up a situation in which there is no other solution; straightforward (honest) male bravery could not save the day.

The Book of Susanna differs from these earlier stories of women tricksters, precisely because Susanna does not trick; Daniel tricks for her. Indeed, we believe that Susanna's un-trickiness furnishes the key to understanding the Book of Susanna. Female trickery cannot resolve the oppositions in the Book of Susanna because female in the story is already fundamentally constructed in opposition to the male Elders. The story of Susanna is so thoroughly a gendered story that if Susanna were to successfully trick, the story would present a compelling model of female strength. A victorious female trickster, in the context of a story that revolves around the theme of gender bifurcation, would be fatal to the legitimacy of male hegemony. Such a message would be unacceptable given the patriarchal cultural context of the story. On the other hand, the story so thoroughly builds up Susanna's piety and faith in God, that she cannot be allowed to lose. That message would be equally unacceptable given the theological context of the story. And so, enter Daniel, the new symbol of transformation. Through Daniel, the story presents the three-part paradigm that anthropologists such as

---

[3] By patriarchy we mean a social system in which women are systematically denied access to socially recognized forms of power. Although members of societies are typically unaware of the underlying social logic by which they live, patriarchy is sometimes made explicit through folkstories and rituals.

48 *The Judgment of Susanna*

Levi-Strauss are fond of uncovering cross-culturally. Daniel, the hypotenuse of the triangle, resolves - like all good tricksters - essentially unreconcilable social forces.

Various writers have considered why trickster-heros are so ubiquitous in folk-tales and myths.[4] Elizabeth Janeway, drawing upon the work of Laura Makarius, points out that "not only is it unsettling to find that a player of tricks is held to be worthy of honor, what is even more remarkable is that he is honored **because** he breaks the sacred law" (1981, 142-143). Janeway explains this seemingly illogical cultural stance in terms of the communal good. "In the trickster myths... power is not being sought just for the aggrandizement of the hero, but also (in the end) for a purpose related to the whole community" (Janeway 1981, 143).

Applying Janeway's insights to women tricksters in the Bible, we can argue that they, on the whole, trick for communal rather than individual benefits. Running through our list of biblical heroines, we can see that there are two categories of communal goals which are attained by the tricksters. First, a number of tricksters deceive someone who would bequeath the inheritance of the line on the "wrong" person. The best example here is of course Rebecca, who pulls a rather dirty fast one on her old and ailing husband, and tricks him into giving his blessing to the younger son. Yet Rebecca's trick is, in the final analysis, consistent with the "true" values of the society: She has lied and tricked for the public good, and thus is not condemned. Second, a group of tricksters deceive someone who would kill or destroy the Israelite people. The best example here is Yael, who enters the story for the sole purpose of tricking Sisera into drinking a soporific so that she can kill him, and thus deprive him and his armies of victory. Again, not only is Yael's deception not censured, she is poetically eulogized as the most noble and beautiful of women.

Despite the culturally sanctioned and clearly well-known option of female trickery, Susanna does not avail herself of this popular female option. The first part of the Book of Susanna sets up a perfect stage for trickery, yet not only does Susanna not trick anybody, she is a passive witness to other people's tricks. In the Book of Susanna the men pull the tricks: the Elders trick her and Daniel tricks the Elders.

We would argue that what distinguishes Susanna from the biblical female tricksters mentioned above is the theme of control over female sexuality (rather than proper inheritance or tribal survival). When the issue at stake is something

---

[4] In particular, anthropologists have written a great deal about American Indian trickster myths. According to Radin (1972), the trickster is an ambivalent figure who serves to reflect the difficulty in resolving the problem of good and evil. The American Indian myth always makes the trickster out to be a loser. Even when the trickster tries to do good, it ends up a loser in a world where good never totally reigns. Daniel is a different kind of trickster. The Book of Susanna presents trickery which supports and bolsters a system which, unlike that of the Indians, presumes that moral order is possible and that everything turns out for the best.

other than a woman's personal autonomy, patriarchal culture is able to allow women a certain amount of latitude to maneuver as independent individuals, particularly when they maneuver in service of the ultimate "good" of the system. When the issue at stake is sexuality, even the "weak power" of trickery is unacceptable.

Coming as a later book than the rest of the Bible, Susanna can be seen as a commentary on both sexuality and trickery in the Bible; it sets out to clarify the limits of women's power. Significantly, other biblical women do not escape rape: Dinah, the Concubine at Gibeah, Tamar. Only Susanna escapes rape, though through no power of her own. In other words, if a biblical man chooses to rape a woman there are only two possible endings to the story: she is raped or a wise saintly man saves her, but she is not allowed to save herself. For better of for worse, men control women's sexuality. From this point of view, the Book of Susanna is a precursor of Cinderella, Sleeping Beauty, and Little Red Riding Hood - the passive and beautiful heroine is saved by Prince Charming (Daniel), not by her own strength.

To reiterate, we posit a link between Susanna's two biblically exceptional traits - she is not a trickster and she escapes rape. Unlike other biblical heroines, Susanna relinquishes the trickster role and invites Daniel to pick up the trickster mantle. Unlike other biblical heroines, Susanna avoids sexual assault. The message is hard to miss - in order to win public support for escaping male sexual violence, Susanna has to forego the one tactic (trickery) which in the biblical context was available to women who function to uphold the moral order.

SEXUAL VIOLENCE

In view of the Susanna story, a question that begs to be asked is why it is necessary for patriarchy to exercise control over a woman's sexuality? And why does patriarchy use sexual violence as a crucial means of controlling women? Although these questions lie somewhat beyond the scope of this paper, we would like to suggest a few possible answers.

We refer here to Ruth Bleier's analysis of sexuality as the "kingpin in the patriarchal formations that serve to oppress women" (1984, 164). Bleier argues that underlying all forms of patriarchal oppression - political, economic, religious - "are the assumptions of the institution of heterosexuality or heterosexism: specifically, the assumptions that men own and have the right to control the bodies, labor, and minds of women" (1984, 164). She contends that sex, partly because of its association with intimacy and love, "is by its very physical nature the most seductive, private, intrusive, direct, and possessing way to exert power and control" (1984, 181). Bleier shows how western religion and western medicine and psychoanalysis have served to master women's sexuality in the interests of male dominance. Both sets of institutions establish, express, embody, or enforce "a set of power relationships between the participants: one, the authority who compels, questions, prescribes, judges, punishes, forgives, deciphers, and interprets; and the subject who sins, speaks, and receives interpreted truth" (1984, 177). The case of Susanna illustrates Bleier's point: The Elders compel, Daniel interprets, and her husband eventually forgives.

There are three aspects of male control of women's sexuality that Bleier sees as especially significant. First, from a young age girls are taught to be appealing to men (recall that the whole episode starts when Susanna's maid goes to bring her creams and oils). Second, from a young age girls are taught to fear rape (Susanna's fear of rape is so great that she prefers public disgrace and execution). And third, violent sex is used as a means of punishing women who "get out of line" sexually or who otherwise disobey or displease men. Cross-culturally rape is used when women, in ways defined by a specific culture, step out of line. In Melanesia this might mean venturing out of the house alone, an act which leaves a woman open to culturally sanctioned group rape. In the United States this might mean accepting a ride home from a fellow student or worker. The combination of violence and sexuality hammers home a message of gender-specific social control: the victim is physically restrained in a manner uniquely and inexorably associated with her gender.

The Book of Susanna, like many other well-known myths (see Brownmiller 1975, esp. Chapter 9 "The Myth of the Heroic Rapist") helps mystify the source of sexual violence against women. Returning to our list of binary equations, we can now tie in one trait which we glossed over earlier - Susanna's beauty. The significance of Susanna's beauty is quite simply to "seduce" the reader into thinking that rape is a consequence of male sexual arousal precipitated by female beauty, rather than a product of culturally condoned patriarchal control of female autonomy; a popular title for the story is actually "The Seduction of Susanna." As Susan Brownmiller has shown, cultural myths teach both men and women to expect that men will not be able to control their "lust" in the presence of female beauty and that women have no independent recourse when confronted with sexual violence - that women "ask for it".

The Israelite attitude toward rape[5] is spelled out in the Pentateuch (see Trible 1984 on rape stories in the Bible). If a virgin were raped outside the city walls, the rapist was ordered to pay the woman's father compensation (bride

---

[5] One could claim that the story of Susanna does not concern rape **according to Jewish legal definitions of what constitutes rape.** Instead, it concerns adultery, sexual coercion, or sexual blackmail. We refer the reader to Susan Brownmiller's critique of patriarchal definitions of rape in which she demonstrates that many cultures officially define rape as a property crime of man against man (woman is the damaged or stolen property). Brownmiller argues that such definitions are useless in terms of understanding and recognizing women's experiences (1975:8ff) .

price) and the two were ordered to marry (Deuteronomy 22:28-29).[6] And if the rape victim belonged to an enemy group (as in the retribution scene in the story of Dinah), rape was treated as a legitimate way for men to breed slaves or acquire concubines. In none of these instances was rape unambiguously condemned - rape served a "legitimate" social function of limiting women's freedom of movement and of annexing human resources to a man's tribe, lineage or household.

In the Book of Susanna - unlike in other biblical stories - the Elders do not get away with threatening to rape Susanna. And Susanna - unlike other biblical rape victims - does not seem to have done anything to elicit male reprisal - she has not stepped out of line (even the garden she walks in belongs to her husband - underscoring her lack of autonomous mobility).[7] Quite to the contrary, the Elders are publicly condemned, humiliated, and executed, and Susanna is portrayed as modest and pious. Still, and this is the crucial point, Susanna's acquittal does not endow her with autonomy, it simply returns her to the home of the husband who accepted the word of the Elders when they accused his wife of adultery. Susanna indeed escapes rape, yet in the Book of Susanna the threat of rape successfully carries its message of patriarchal social control.

A CONTINUING STORY

Our discussion in this paper has been a-historical; we have offered a structural interpretation of the Book of Susanna with little regard to the historical context in which the story was composed. We believe that our a-historical approach reflects the a-historicity of the Book itself. Unlike most other biblical stories, the text does not say in what town the story took place, despite the fact that the town is pertinent to the social setting of the story. The Elders are unnamed - they are presented as paradigmatic bad leaders and anonymous lustful men; they have neither redeeming character traits nor individual personality quirks. The name of the hero - Daniel - translates quite simply as "God's judge" - again, a role title rather than a personal name, given his part in the story. Susanna also is presented as an archetypical figure; she is too flawless - rich and beautiful

---

[6] The Bible does not entertain the possibility that the raped woman would not want to marry the man who raped her. According to Rachel Biale, "First, it was assumed that the woman would wish to marry the man because she has been 'compromised' so that her chances of finding another husband are very slim. Second, rape is not perceived here as a sadistic or perverse act, but rather as a socially improper way of taking a wife" (Biale 1984:242-243). Later Rabbinic rulings took into account the possibility that the woman might not wish to marry the man who had raped her (Biale 1984:239-255).

[7] It is not clear in the text that Susanna has stepped out of line, although it may be possible that the high socio-economic status or her extreme piety bothered the Elders. Later interpretations of the story "correct" this deficiency. Ellen Spolsky shows that in certain Renaissance paintings Susanna is portrayed as self-absorbed with her own beauty, see p. 103.

and brave and pious. Like the unnamed "woman" in Song of Songs and like Eve, Susanna - whose name means "lily" - is found in a garden. We concur with Harold Fisch's suggestion that the Book of Susanna should be seen as a parable on the Song of Songs: Susanna is indeed a "lily among thorns."[8] We believe that the absence of individual names for the main characters in the Book of Susanna, together with the too perfect binary oppositions discussed earlier, serves to imply that the story is a moral and legal parable, and not a historical anecdote. On the other hand, the cultural contexts in which the Book of Susanna has been read and re-told are discernible. In the final section of this paper we turn our attention to the question of why the Book of Susanna never became popular in Jewish tradition, whereas among Christians - at least certain groups of Christians - Susanna became one of the best-known biblical women.

As we have argued, the theme of moral strength vs. structural strength is central to the story of Susanna. Whereas this theme resonates strongly within Christian traditions, it is at most a peripheral theme in Jewish tradition. We have already shown that other biblical heroines do not serve as prototypes for Susanna. Susanna's unequivocal structural weakness and undiluted moral strength - remember that she does not even trick - is a combination not found in any earlier biblical heroines, nor is it picked up on in later Jewish stories. When one thinks of the Jewish heroines who lived in the centuries after Susanna, it is clear that Susanna (or the Susanna-type combination of moral strength and structural weakness) was not a pivotal image.[9] Our argument here is two-fold: neither is the structural strength vs. moral strength scenario endemic to Jewish culture (Jewish heros, like David and Abraham, encompass good and bad, strength and weakness), nor is moral strength and structural weakness particularly associated with women in Jewish tradition.[10]

In contrast, within Christian tradition structural weakness **is** a frequent companion of moral strength, and this combination is often assigned to women. Indeed, Susanna and Susanna-type women became the prototypes of Christian martyrdom (Boitani, this volume). This argument (without specific mention of Susanna) has recently been developed in Shari Horner's study of 9th century Anglo-Saxon nuns' predilection for the story of the 4th century virgin martyr Juliana. Horner's structuralist analysis of the Old English poem *Juliana* is strikingly similar to our analysis of the Book of Susanna. "Early in the poem a number of oppositions emerge. Most obviously, the Christian **Juliana** is

---

[8] See above, p. 35.

[9] The best-known woman of the Talmud, Beruriah, is a mirror image of Susanna. In the Talmud she is presented as assertive, articulate, forceful and educated. However, Rashi relates a story of her having committed adultery with one of her husband's pupils (see Lacks 1980: 129ff. for a feminist analysis of the story of Beruriah).

[10] We speak broadly of Jewish and Christian "tradition" and "culture." Although Jewish and Christian cultures have existed in myriad forms, on different continents, and throughout different eras, we do believe that there is a structural logic or integrity which underlies the various manifestations of Jewish and Christian traditions.

juxtaposed with the pagan **men**. Within this dichotomy are others: the use of **private** oaths ... versus **public** declarations[11]...; the **material** versus the **spiritual** (Juliana specifically rejects Eleusius's wealth in favor of God's love); physical **violence** versus spiritual **calm** .... The emphasis on the men's physicality culminates when they meet: their voices rose up ... as they leaned their spears together" (1994: 665, our emphases). Horner in fact contrasts the Susanna-like Christian Juliana to one of the "tricky" Jewish heroines we mentioned earlier. "The recourse a nun might have against the threat of physical violation is precisely developed in the discourse of [monastic] enclosure: because she cannot hope to win a physical battle against pagan invaders (**in spite of the model of Judith**), she can only fight the spiritual battle to keep her body enclosed and inviolate" (1994: 671-672, our emphasis). Juliana, like Susanna, is indeed different from Judith and Old Testament heroines.

According to Brock and Harvey, "Christian literature has painted the experience of martyrdom and persecution as far more extreme than generally happened" (1987, 15). In these martyrdom stories one sees dramatically that "the battle between good and evil is here at work" (1987: 17) and good is often associated with women who are victims of sexual violence or even mutilation (1987: 24). The impetus for these hyperboles is theological - *imitatio Christi*; stories of moral strength and structural weakness resonate not only with key events in Christian history, but also with pivotal theological stances. One could argue that the essential Christian moral stance, as expounded by Jesus in the Sermon of the Mount, is a stance of binary oppositions, of moral strength, and structural strength. If the meek inherit the earth and rich men cannot enter heaven, martyred women - and Susanna - perfectly embody Christian creed. As women writers from St. Hildegard on have claimed, the very weakness of women makes them especially appropriate spiritual vessels (Newman 1987).

Brock and Harvey raise another point which is crucial to our discussion. They show that although early Christian women martyrs often broke with cultural norms of proper female behavior, this was acceptable because, "the duty of the Christian to act according to God's will thus allowed a continual but anomalous position of authority for holy women" (1987: 22-23). Christian martyrs were condoned for behavior that otherwise would not be permissible for women (they were active, noisy, and public figures) even though the threat typically appeared focused upon their individual sexual freedom (either their refusal to marry, or sexual violation and mutilation at the hands of pagan torturers), rather than upon any apparent communal good. In Christian Susanna-type stories, the heroine is applauded for demanding control over her own body. This motif is inconsistent with earlier Jewish texts; recall our suggestion that Susanna could not trick because the issue at stake was her own bodily integrity rather than survival of the lineage or community.

---

[11] For the nuns privacy meant architectural enclosure within cloisters, reminiscent, to our mind, of the walled garden in the Susanna story.

Moreover, given the theological significance of virginity in certain Christian contexts,[12] one can interpret these stories, like the Jewish women trickster stories, not as tales of women freeing themselves of patriarchal control but as tales of women acting for the greater communal good. As Virginia Burrus has pointed out, "The culturally dominant androcentric construction of virginal sexuality, which crystallizes out of the distinctive needs of the post-Constantinian church, functions to create and defend new communal boundaries and to reassert and strengthen the gender hierarchy" (1995:51).[13] In other words, Burrus seems to be arguing, in line with Bleier's and Brownmiller's ideas, that sexual violence - even in the framework of stories that ostensibly condemn the perpetrators, can serve to bolster patriarchy.

CONCLUSION

Despite Susanna's victory over the Elders, the story of Susanna functions to maintain patriarchy, not undermine it. From that point of view, the Susanna story is consonant with both Jewish and Christian traditions. Still, we suggest that Susanna differs in significant ways from female protagonists of both traditions, and should be viewed as a transitional figure. As we have shown, she is sufficiently unlike traditional Jewish heroines as to elicit almost no Jewish recognition. Her story more closely resembles the Christian virgin martyr stories (the Book of Susanna of course pre-dates these stories), accounting for her greater popularity in Christian culture. Nonetheless, Susanna does not fully fit the Christian virgin martyr prototype either (the Book is, after all, a Jewish text). Not only was she far more passive than women like Juliana, but she agreeably returned to her husband at the end of the story - a finale inconsistent with virgin martyrologies.[14] Put differently, the **contextualization** of the gendered plot in the story of Susanna reflects Jewish culture: Susanna's body is significant in terms of lineage and law.[15] However, the **binary structure** of the gendered plot with its special emphasis upon female bodily integrity is

---

[12] See Peter Brown's (1988) comprehensive study of the body in the early Church.

[13] Burrus speculates that ascetic women themselves may not have shared this view; instead, seeing in virginity liberation from male attempts to control women's sexuality, social relationships, and intellectual strivings (1994: 51).

[14] In comparing Jewish and Christian exegesis of procreation in the Garden of Eden story, Gary Anderson comments that, "Because Christians believed that the next world was devoid of marriage (Luke 20:27-40), it followed that the Garden was as well.... Rabbinic Judaism, on the other hand, did not have a high regard for the celibate condition.... The act of human procreation was not simply an acceptable act, it was a **commanded** act" (1992: 47). Whereas early Christian discourse about women's bodies centered upon the question of whether sexuality of any kind is acceptable, Jewish discourse from the same period focused upon the types and circumstances of acceptable sexuality.

[15] The text mentions not only her husband, but her father, mother, children, and "all her kindred."

more congruent with Christian theology and institutions. Susanna's transitional nature may well explain why she has on the one hand remained a fairly marginal character, and why she has on the other hand continued to intrigue artists, writers, musicians, and anthropologists.

It is fitting perhaps that we end this paper with thoughts regarding the figure who emerges as the true, if rather enigmatic, hero in the story of Susanna - Daniel. In the Book, Daniel publicly adopts a role that, as we have seen, was a typical role for biblical heroines - trickster. We posit three possible explanations. First, Daniel's trickery highlights Susanna's lack of trickery: Daniel's tricking the Elders indicates that the writer of the story knew very well that trickery is a legitimate and recognized power of the weak, but that he has chosen not to offer this power to Susanna. Daniel's use of trickery simply reinforces Susanna's passivity. Second, we suspect that Susanna cannot use trickery because to do so, in the context of this essentially gendered story, would be to rebel against the very foundation of patriarchy - male control of women's bodily autonomy. Daniel's trickery is needed to "prove" that what is being fiddled with in the story is the laws of witnesses and not patriarchy. And finally, if we take seriously the end (the punchline) of the story, we understand that this story is essentially about the debut of a leader who incorporates both male and female strengths: structural weakness (Daniel is an outsider), moral superiority, trickery, articulateness, access to the public sphere, youth, and legal knowledge. Given the setting of the Book of Susanna in Babylonia rather than in Israel, it may well be that Daniel was mythically constructed as a figure who could lead his own community in a situation in which that community was politically subordinate. So in the end the Elders were put to death, Susanna passively returned to her family, and Daniel - synthesizing or co-opting the powers of both Susanna and the Elders - emerges as the model of a Diaspora leader.

False Witness and the Just Use of Evidence in The Wycliffite *Pistel of Swete Susan*

David Lyle Jeffrey
University of Ottawa

The Middle English Alliterative poem *The Pistel of Swete Susan* well illustrates the old maxim that a good tale may serve many purposes. Surviving in five MS versions, the 14th century English poem by an unknown northerner named Huchown (Hutcheon) seems to have been of widespread popularity in its own time.[1]

There were numerous ways for English readers in the age of Chaucer to know the story: besides the Vulgate text in Daniel 13, read as the epistle for Saturday in the third week of Lent (hence the "Pistel" of our vernacular title), there existed several medieval Latin poems, the most proximate of which is the curiously erudite version of Alan de Melsa, a Cistercian monk of Beverly, written about 1300.[2] The story features also in Petrus Riga's *Biblia Versificata* (or *Aurora*), and is translated in the Wycliffite Bible.[3] Whether Chaucer, who alludes to Susanna in his Man of Law's Tale (1.639) and possibly Merchant's

---

[1] In her edition, *Susanna: Alliterative Poem of the Fourteenth Century* (New Haven: Yale University Press, 1969), Alice Miskimin gives a full account of the five ME manuscripts, with a generous discussion of variants.

[2] Melsa's poem, edited with two others on the subject, by J.H. Mozley, "Susanna and the Elders: Three Medieval Poems," *Studi Medievali*, n.s. 3 (1930), 27-52, begins with an account of the writer's own conversion and vocation, then goes on to narrate the poem with specific focus on moral lessons for five groups: women, old men, youths, judges and witnesses. Melsa's poem (418 lines) is rife with spurious allusion to classical myth not in any way followed by the *Pistel*, and is traditionally allegorical; his greatly elaborated garden could conceivably have been an influence.

[3] Peter Riga's text gives the *Historia Susanne* according to the rearrangement and elaboration of Aegidius of Paris with an *allegoria* by the same writer, ed. Paul E. Beichner, C.S.C., *Aurora: Petri Rigae Biblia Versificata*, 2 vols. (Notre Dame: Notre Dame University Press, 1965). The Wycliffite Bible is edited in 4 vols. by Rev. Josiah Forshall and Sir Fredric Madden (Oxford, 1850).

57

Tale[4] had contact with the *Pistel of Swete Susan* or merely the Vulgate or Wycliffite Bible version we are not able to say. But that his Parson, if indeed he were a "Loller," could have imagined that the story of Susanna was a text for the times -- times, it might seem, of impending persecution -- is at least a plausible imagination. It is an emotionally aroused "poor priest" who declares:

> Ware yow, questemongeres [lawyers] and notaries!
> Certes, for fals witnessyng was Susanna in ful
> gret sorwe and peyne, <u>and</u> <u>many</u> <u>another</u> <u>mo</u>.[5]

Whether Chaucer's Parson was a Wycliffite sympathizer or not, it is evident that the *Pistel of Swete Susan* (written within a decade of his sermon) is an identifiably Lollard narration, a theologically charged retelling of the remarkable detective story first associated with the book of Daniel.[6]

The first thing a student of biblical literary tradition looks for in a retelling such as this is the character of any variations from the source text. On first glance the ME poem in substantial measure parallels the Vulgate and, although here in only rudimentary plot outline, the three major Latin poems based upon it. All of these, following the decision taken by St. Jerome during his translation of the Vulgate, are indebted to the version of Theodotion rather than that of the LXX, except for certain implications arising from the matter of Jerome's placement of it at the end of Daniel.[7] The *Pistel* has, however, its own distinctive elements of emphatic narrative elaboration. Some of these, such as the beautifully aureated garden description, the betrayal of Susanna at mid-day when she stops under a laurel ("lorer") tree to bathe, and, after the charge against her is laid down, the mature intimacy of the audience she requests with her husband, all seem designed to establish narrative and even

---

    [4] See Alfred L. Kellogg, "Susanna and the Merchant's Tale," *Speculum* 35 (1960), 275-79.

    [5] The Parson's vehemence of feeling on this issue is transparent (798-9). It is Harry Bailey, the Host of the Canterbury pilgrimage, who calls him a "Loller" (Epilogue to the Tale of the Man of Law, 1173-77).

    [6] Dorothy Sayers includes the Vulgate "Susanna" along with Daniel 14, the apocryphal "Bel and the Dragon," as the first two tales in her anthology of mystery stories, *Omnibus of Crime* (London, 1929).

    [7] The LXX version is longer, enriching the trial scene with Susanna's four children and five hundred servants as well as the appearance of angels. Theodotion's version places the narrative where chronologically it makes sense, as ch. 1 of Daniel, and emphasizes both the garden scene and the contrast between Daniel's youth (like Jesus with the elders in the Temple, he had just turned 12) and the *senectute in malo* of the corrupt judges. See R.H. Charles, *The Apocrypha and Pseudepigrapha of the Old Testament*, 2 vols. (Oxford: Black, 1912), 1.638ff. The *Peshitta* agrees most closely with Theodotion, except that Susanna's soliloquy and her repudiation of the elders are both expanded.

theological resonance with other biblical texts.[8] Other elaborations, however, such as the praise of her parents for having educated her to literacy in the "letter" and "theology" of "moises," or the suggestion that there is heightened, even heroic humanity in those who maintain patient fidelity in the face of unjust prosecution, can safely be regarded as of central importance to a Wycliffite poet and a late 14th century audience with Wycliffite sympathies. And there are other, teasing connections to the manorial circle of the so-called "Lollard Knights."[9] But this is merely to scratch the surface.

If a medieval Christian went to church on the Saturday before the third Sunday in Lent -- something members of the established and emerging class families of 14th century English "Lollard knights" might likely do -- he or she would hear read as the epistle for that day the entire account of Susanna from

---

[8] The elaborate garden recalls, of course, both the lover's garden in Song of Songs (Canticle of Solomon) and its medieval descendants, including the conflation with Eden in the *Roman de la Rose*. But there is a patristic precedent for connecting Susanna and Joachim's garden both to Eden and that in the Song of Songs: St. Ambrose, noting that Susanna in Hebrew means "lily" (cf. *Pistel*, 16, where the ME poet shows knowledge of this etymology), compares her innocence or purity to that of Christ as a "lily among thorns" in the *hortus conclusus* allegory (Cant. 2:1.2). This innocence is a lily, he says, "which loves to grow in gardens, in which Susanna, while walking, found it, and was ready to die rather than it should be violated." A notable feature of the poem which it is possible here only briefly to indicate, is the extra dimension given to the marriage relationship by the *Pistel* poet, especially prominent in the moments after Susanna's sentence of death (244-60), lines which heighten the reader's appreciation of the great nobility of character in both spouses. If this poem had as its original patrons a distinguished couple, this might have been regarded as a tribute to their own marriage.

[9] Russell A. Peck in his recent edition of the text, "The Pistel of Swete Susan" (pp. 73-108 in *Heroic Women from the Old Testament in Middle English Verse*) agrees with A.I. Doyle that a signature in the margin of the so-called Simeon MS (British Museum MS Additional 22, 283) might be that of Joan Bohun, at once sister of Archbishop Thomas Arundel and wife to Humphrey Bohun, Earl of Hereford. One of her daughters owned a Wycliffite Bible; she herself was an exceptionally pious woman for whom Doyle thinks the Vernon MS (including a copy of the *Pistel of Swete Susan*) might well have been commissioned. See A.I. Doyle, "The Shaping of the Vernon and Simeon Manuscripts," in *Chaucer and Middle English Studies in Honor of Rossell Hope Robbins*, ed. Beryl Rowland (Kent: Kent State University Press, 1974), 328-41. But almost any of the pious noble households associated with the so-called "Lollard knights" -- men like Sir William Neville, Sir John Clanvowe, Sir Lewis Clifford, Sir Roger Stury would be as likely. And another Joan, Joan of Kent, widow of Edward III's heroic older brother, the Black Prince, herself regarded as the most beautiful lady of all England and an apparent supporter and intimate of the Lollard knight circle, would be as suitable to the elegant compliment the *Pistel of Swete Susan* would make if offered to her patronage. See D.L. Jeffrey, "Chaucer and Wyclif: Biblical Hermeneutic and Literary Theory in the XIVth Century," in *Chaucer and Scriptural Tradition* (Ottawa: University of Ottawa Press, 1984), 109-142.

Daniel 13.[10]   The epistle would be the first text to be read; after a gradual
psalm, the gospel lection ordained for the day would be John 8:1-11 -- the story
of Jesus and the "woman taken in adultery." The apropos of this traditional
ecclesiastical connection of biblical narratives will appear at once to those
familiar with both stories. In the first, an entirely innocent woman is trapped,
slandered, and condemned to death by stoning according to the Law of Moses
-- then miraculously released and vindicated by a young Daniel "come to
judgment," as Shakespeare has it. In the second narrative, the gospel on which
the sermon (if there was one) would most usually be preached, a presumably
guilty woman is trapped, not primarily for the sake of her accusers' pursuit of
righteousness according to the Law, but rather for their devious purposes of a
further entrapment -- this time of Jesus, who is to be hung on the horns of a
dilemma created by his response to the biblical law concerning adultery. In this
narrative, also miraculously, the woman is released -- though here not because
vindicated but because pardoned.

There are, however, further parallels. In the New Testament account of
the woman taken in adultery there are two distinct parties who bring her before
Jesus en route to her sorry fate; the scribes and the Pharisees (John 8:3). In
Susanna the accusers are also two parties, in this case single individuals, but
who are likewise elders and judges in Israel. In both stories the claim is that
the woman was caught in the "very act" (although there is no more 'empirical'
evidence in the spare Johannine narrative than in Susanna's case actually to
substantiate the claim). In both narratives the accusers move immediately to
press for punishment (John 8:5; Dan. 13:36-41); and in both the right discovery
of blame and due apportioning of justice (and, in John 8, mercy) is
accomplished by one unexpectedly more attuned to the intent of the Law than
the presiding judges (who in the Johannine narrative, if not in Daniel, are also
the accusers[11]). Because the normative way for a medieval Christian to
encounter the Vulgate text of Susanna was as the "Pistel" to which the
Johannine story is the companion "Gospel," it will be clear that the story of the
woman taken in adultery provides an important and vivifying context for a
medieval Christian audience's appreciation of Susanna's peril and deliverance.

At least one contemporary literary text besides the *Pistel of Swete Susan*
-- not of Wycliffite but of likely Franciscan provenance -- suggests how easily
the two narratives might be connected in a popular literary adaptation. In the

---

[10]   Daniel 13 forms the epistle for Saturday before the third Sunday in Lent in both the
Old Sarum and new Roman rite. In some household chapels (see n. 9 above) by the 1390s
the text might conceivably be read from the Wycliffite translation.

[11]   In the Vulgate (Daniel 13:24-41) it appears that the villainous elders both make the
charge and conduct the trial. This, as pointed out by F.J. Amours in his *Scottish Alliterative
Poems 38* (Edinburgh: Scottish Text Society, 1897), 377, would be contrary to English law,
in which the accuser cannot be the judge -- hence in the *Pistel* other justices are introduced.
Lyra in his gloss seems to have assumed the same thing, however.

Ludus Coventriae (N-Town) play of "The Woman Taken in Adultery"[12] (24) a character is added to the biblical source called simply Juvenis, or young man. When apprehended with the woman (Mulier) he threatens his two captors (Scriba and Phariseus) and, because they fear his strength and also because, as is soon to become clear, they are themselves implicated in a double standard, they let him go. The comic function afforded by his taunting escape speeches aside (ll. 127-144), the invented character himself is clearly indebted to the accusatory invention of the two false witnesses in Daniel 13, who, we remember, posit a young man too strong for them to prevent him escaping out the garden door.

It is virtually certain that neither Wyclif nor any of his followers, despite their heightened appreciation for certain theologically significant properties of the Hebrew language, had direct knowledge of the *Mishnah* (i.e. Sotah 1-3) or of Talmudic commentary. Neither would they likely have had access to the various 14th and 15th century Hebrew versions.[13] But because Jerome's biblical commentaries were a favorite source -- indeed, Jerome's prologues were translated (perhaps by John Purvey) in the prologue of the Wycliffite Bible -- literate Wycliffite adherents would have known at a minimum that Jerome accepted traditional rabbinic association of the two corrupt elders with the tyrannous and adulterous false prophets Ahab and Zedekiah of Jeremiah 29:20-23.[14] Moreover, the extant corpus of vernacular Wycliffite sermons and tracts shows that their authors were much better versed in the actual text of the Old Testament (Torah especially) than most of their English contemporaries,

---

[12] Ed. K.S. Block, *Ludus Coventriae or The Plaie called Corpus Christi*, EETS e.s. 120 (Oxford: Oxford University Press, 1922; 1960), 200-209.
[13] R.H. Charles (1.644) believes there are many of these. See the essay by Betsy Halpern-Amaru above. R. Brull, *Das apokryphische Susanna-Buch* (1877) said that Nachmani was the only medieval Jewish author of note to make significant mention of Susanna (6). Rabbi Brull attributes composition of Susanna to the times of Simon Ben Shetach, who was president of the Sanhedrin about 100 B.C.E. Simon is known to have advocated the rigid cross-examination of witnesses (*Pirke Aboth* 1.9-10). "He also urged that those found guilty of perjury should be punished with the penalty appointed for the crime with which they had falsely accused another": see H. Maldwyn Hughes, *The Ethics of Jewish Apocryphal Literature* (London: Robert Culley, 1910), 68-69. This position was opposed by the Sadducees, who held for capital punishment only when the betrayed innocent had already been put to death. Their quarrel is the situation which lies behind the strange and disturbing story of the preventable execution of Simon's son (*Pirke Aboth* 1.9).
[14] They are not, nevertheless, so named in the ME poem. The association with Jeremiah, however, greatly encourages their transformation in the *Pistel* to "preosts," and it is of relevance here also that Jeremiah's rant against despoiling priests provides much of the textual support and practical rhetoric for Wycliffite denunciation of corrupt or worldly clergy in their own day. The gloss in the Wycliffite Bible seems to reflect Jer. 23:20-23 when it says, at v. 56, "This iuge was of Canaan bi condiciouns, since he diseyuede wymmen bi ferdfulnesse." (The association with Jeremiah occurs one way or another in Midrash Tanhuma on Leviticus; Sanhedrin 93a [Babylonian Talmud]; R. Eliezer, Boraitha c33; and Pesikta 25.)

and hence it is not unusual for them to reveal awareness of biblical provisions concerning such cases, both with respect to penalties (e.g., Deut. 19:15-19; Lev. 20:10) and procedures (Num. 5:11-31; Lev. 24:14). It is in virtue of their own commitment to what the Susanna poet calls the "maundement of Moises," or what Wyclif himself calls *Legem Moysii, Lex Dei*[15] that the terrible nature of the dilemma in Susanna's entrapment (as, in a different fashion, that of the woman in John 8) would be agonizingly clear to them. But so also, I want to suggest, would their appreciation of the unexpected judge's resolution make sense in terms of the law as they knew it in its biblical context.

It is not necessary to argue for more than their familiarity with the Bible on these points. It may be, as Lightfoot suggests, that in the case of the woman taken in adultery Jesus was making inferential use of a rabbinic caveat on the provisions of Num. 5 to the effect that the adulterous woman shall receive her punishment only if the "husband" be guiltless of iniquity (Sanhedrin 51.2; Maimonides on Sotah 2-3) or invoking in his script in the sand another version of the general principle enunciated by the Bemidbar Rabba that "If you follow whoring yourselves, the bitter waters will not try your wives" (235). However apropos such a reading might be, English Wycliffites could not have known it.[16] Indeed, in the Wycliffite sermon on the passage, the final gospel for Saturday the third week in Lent, the author specifically abjures speculation concerning what Jesus wrote in the sand.[17] But concerning the method by which Daniel convicts the lecherous elders in Susanna there was plenty of ordinary biblical warrant. Deuteronomy mandates the specific requisite of a "diligent inquisition" in the case of possible false witness (Deut. 19:18), and it is evident in Daniel 13 that the presiding judges were partial to the lecherous elders in failing to "enquire carefully and diligently into the truth of the thing by looking well into it" (Deut. 13:14). It may be the case, as Hastings has suggested, that Dan. 13 affords one of the earliest examples of cross-examination in legal history, but the principle certainly predates this

---

[15] For Wyclif the whole of Scripture is the *legem Dei*. But he and his followers often refer to the Old Testament globally as the *legem Moysii*; among Wycliffite adherents Wyclif and his intimate colleagues are referred to, especially in reference to their teaching the Old Testament, as "sitting in Moses' chair." See, e.g. "The Testimony of William Thorpe," ed. Anne Hudson, *Two Wycliffite Texts*, EETS o.s. 301 (Oxford: Oxford University Press, 1993), 41. The ability of Wycliffite defendants to show a detailed and astute knowledge of biblical law is evident throughout these and similar texts.

[16] John Lightfoot, *Commentary on the New Testament from the Talmud and Hebraica*, 4 vols. (Oxford: Oxford University Press, 1859; rpr. Peabody, Mass.: Hendrickson, 1989), 1.325-332.

[17] Ed. Anne Hudson, *English Wycliffite Sermons*, 4 vols. (Oxford: Oxford University Press, 1987-1995), 3.125-128, Sermon no. 164, *Sabato iij Septimane Quadragesime Sermo 43*. Lyra in this case demurs. For him, in his *Glossa* it is plausible to think that Christ wrote on the ground the incriminating sins of the woman's accusers: "*Alii dicunt, et melius ut videtur, quod scriberat eorum peccata, ut eos ostenderet ineptos ad accusiationem hujus foeminae.*"

narrative in Jewish law, and the pertinent biblical law receives significant comment in Wycliffite writings.[18] Wycliffite authors had as well their own "midrash," their canon of preferred commentators on both narrative and legal matters in the biblical text. Besides Jerome, chief among those employed by John Purvey in his completion of the Wycliffite translation of the Bible were Thomas Aquinas and Nicholas of Lyra, "especially on the Old Testament."[19] Lyra is everywhere cited by Wyclif himself as the modern commentator most to be trusted, and Aquinas (with whom Wyclif had sided against the Scotists and whom he credits with pointing him back to Augustine) is relied upon by Wyclif especially in the area of moral and civil law (e.g. *De domino civilo*).

The pertinence of Lyra to the Middle English Susanna attaches first of all to her characterization as an exemplum for faithful believers in a time of persecution. Lyra (who was thought by virtue of his command of Hebrew to have been Jewish by birth), regards the Susanna story for its deeply thoughtful morality, seeing it as a story which is of exemplary value in part because the problem of false accusation is not limited to the past.[20] But following Jerome, Lyra also sees in Susanna under attack a figure of true rather than merely circumstantial nobility: it is not on account of her family's wealth or her own good looks but rather on account of the character formed because her parents chose to have her instructed in the Law (*parentes autem illius eum essent iusti erudierent filiam suam secundum legem moysi*) that she acquires this true gentility. In his own commentary on Daniel 13, Jerome had in fact begun by stressing (perhaps more than the text can bear) the virtue of her parents having "instructed" Susanna "according to the law of Moses," extrapolating a defense for one of his own unconventional practices, teaching women: the verse is included, he says, to exhort parents to teach not only their sons but also their daughters according to the Law of God (*ut doceant iuxta legem Dei sermonemque divinum non solum filios sed et filias suas*).[21] This became a cardinal point also for the Wycliffites (Jerome's exhortation appears as a gloss on Susanna in their translation)[22] and it grounded a practice which aroused the

---

[18] *Dictionary of the Bible*, ed. J. Hastings, 4 vols. (London and New York: T.T. Clark, 1902), 4.630-32. Such Wycliffite texts as "The Testimony of William Thorpe" and "Wycliffe's Apology" locate the justification for cross-examination in Deuteronomy.

[19] See Purvey's prologue in Forshall and Madden, 1.57.

[20] Supra Dn. XIII, "*In hoc autem capitulo ipsius Susanne falsa ponitur accusatio. et in casu simili accusatio habet aliquam veritas apparentiam ex duobus....*"

[21] Supra Danielem XIII, in Francisci Glorie, ed. *Commentariorum in Danielem Libri III* (IV). S. Hieronymi Presbyteri Opera, Pars 1, Opera Exegetica 5. Corpus Christianorum Series Latina 75A (Brepols: Turnholt, 1964), 995. This entirely accords with his comments in his preface to Galatians and his famous letter to the Roman matron Laetitia (Epist. 107; cf. Epist. 52).

[22] Supra 13.3, "tau3ten her doutir" -- "*here fadris and modris ben monestid to teche bi the lawe of God, not only her sones, but also her dou3tris.*"

ire of their more misogynist ecclesiastical accusers; Wyclif's chief colleague John Purvey, they charged, went so far as to write a book advocating the propriety of women teaching Scripture.[23] That the *Pistel of Swete Susan* should begin as it does, stressing the educated moral intelligence of Susanna, is consistent with this Wycliffite theme and its lineage of commentators.

To the Middle English poet it seems entirely fitting that Joachim also be characterized as noble, not merely, as in the Vulgate text, for his riches and status, but for gracious rectitude of his personal character: he too is "a Jeuw jentil... so lele in his lawe ther lived non him liche" (2-3). Susan, a product of her parents' instruction in Scripture, is veritably a kind of Lady Chokma or "Wis-dam" as the Wycliffite Bible calls her (cf. Prov. 31), possessed not only of a knowledge of the Law itself, but also of a clear-headed theology. Joachim is accordingly a man blessed, for their relationship is rich in intellectual as well as physical intimacy:

> He hed a wif hight Susan, was sotil and sage:
> Heo was Elches doughter, eldest and eyre,
> Lovelich and lilie whit, on of that lynage,
> Of alle fason of foode frelich and feire.
> Thei lerned hire lettrure of that langage:
> The maundement of Moises they marked to that may,
> To the mount of Synai that went in message
> That the Trinite bitok of tables a peire
>   To rede.
> Thus thei lerne hire the lawe
> Cleer clergye to knawe;
> To God stod hire gret awe,
>   That wlonkest in weede. (14-26)

The connection of true gentility with faithfulness to God's Law (cf. Chaucer's lyric "Gentilesse") is a familiar one to readers of Wycliffite texts from this period. For example, the Wycliffite exposition of the *Ave Maria* is preoccupied with the issue of a decaying gentility ("sumtyme curtesie & gentrie was vertuouse lif & honest in word & dede & alle manere of good berynge & suster of holynesse"), and urges its female readers to take a leading role in recovering that virtuous civic standard: "O 3e gentil wommen, þenkiþ hou noble wommen & clene & stedefast han be bifore 3ou, as oure lady seynt marie, marie magdaleyne, sussanne... and many moo."[24] We cannot avoid recognizing that for the poem's audience the principal women cited are notable biblical exemplars of "hearers" and "doers" of the Law -- faithful students of

---

[23] See Jeffrey, *The Law of Love: English Spirituality in the Age of Wyclif* (Grand Rapids: Eerdmans, 1988), 44; but cf. Anne Hudson, "John Purvey: A Reconsideration of the Evidence for his Life and Writings," *Viator* 12 (1981), 355-80.

[24] F.D. Matthew, ed. *The English Works of Wyclif*, EETS o.s. 74 (London: Kegan Paul, Trench and Trubner, 1880; 1902), 205.

the Word of God. For medieval and Renaissance painters and MS illustrators Mary is the one to whom comes the incarnate Word because she is found to be one in whose heart the word already is hidden (as medieval paintings of the Annunciation typically declare by having Gabriel find her reading Torah); to the angel's annunciation she replies, "Be it unto me according to thy Word" (Luke 1:38). Mary Magdalene is the one who calls Jesus "Rabbuni" (my teacher), and who sits at the feet of Jesus rather than help her frustrated sister Martha make the blintzes (Luke 10:38-42). Susanna's education in the Law is likewise to be regarded, on the evidence of Wycliffite readings at least, as evidence of her (and her parents) having "chosen the better part."

To summarize on this point: the Wycliffite Susan is not just "taught according to the Law"; she is made to be, like her husband, literate in the Law. For the Wycliffite poem I think, this intensification makes her not only a paragon of the virtues Wycliffites generally believed would accrue to any one who would "with good living and meekness ... study the Bible,"[25] but in this poetic version of her story her mature comprehension of the Law greatly heightens the reader's sense of the dignity and self-possession which subtends her gracious comportment during the ugly proposition of the would-be rapists and the anguish of her formal trial. She knows well enough the law which is being used against her, and that it is not herself only but the Law in question which is being abused. When the leering old men proposition her they say "wolt thu, ladi, for love on ure lay lerne...?" (135): the ME pun on lay (it can mean law, song, and, as in modern English, coitus) is surely a calculated irony on the poet's part.

Wycliffites regarded this abuse of the power of the Law to exploit someone trying to live by the Law (as Lyra's gloss *et in casu simili accusatio habet aliquam veritas* might have suggested), as pretty much their own misfortune. They too, as Wyclif was fond of saying, lived in their own time of "Babylonian captivity," especially after the papal schism and the tumultuous ecclesiastical events of 1378.[26] The so-called "Apology of Wycliffe," also a vernacular tract of the times, the vernacular translation of Wyclif's "Of Prelates" and "The Testimony of William Thorpe" (ostensibly an account of the latter's trial before Archbishop Arundel) all cite Susanna as a model of heroic virtue in the face of false accusation in a time of Babylonian tyranny. Thorpe, for example, finds himself on the horns of a similar dilemma: he fears he will be condemned by God if he should agree with his prosecutors to betray other Wycliffites (and indeed to refrain himself from preaching), yet he is as certain to be condemned by the Archbishop if, like Susanna, he fails to cooperate with

---

[25] Prologue to Wycliffite Bible; Jeffrey, *Law of Love*, 339.

[26] Ibid., 6-7. A quarrel between Pope Urban VI and his French cardinals resulted in their absconding with the papal jewels to Avignon, where they elected a rival pope, the Savoyard Robert of Sicily. This schism, with rival popes at Rome and Avignon, lasted almost 40 years, and did much to undermine the credibility of papal authority in England particularly.

his prosecutors. At first he remembers her stratagem of silence:

> And I heerynge þese wordis þou3te in myn herte þat þis was an vnleeful /
> askynge, and I demed mysilf cursid of God if I consentid herto; and I þou3te
> how Susanne seide 'Angwysschis ben to me on euery side', and forþi þat I
> stood stille musynge and spak not.[27]

In "Of Prelates," which concerns the fate of those (Wycliffite
sympathizers) wrongly "acursed of prelatis," it is typically charged that
whenever "a trewe man displese a worldly prelate for techynge and mentenynge
of goddis lawe" the ecclesiastical authorities

> brynge many false witnesses & notaries in his absence, & in presence speke
> no word, & thei feynen þis false lawe, 3if þre or four false witnesses hirid bi
> money seye sich a þing a3enst a trewe man, þan he schal not be herd, þou3
> he wolde proue þe contrarie bi two hundrid or þre; & þes false men seye in
> here doynge þat crist was lafully don to þe deþ, & susanne also, for bi sich
> witnessis þei weren dampnyd, but cristene men bileue techiþ þe contrarie. &
> bi þis false lawe þei may proue heretikis whom euere þei wolen; 3e, crist &
> alle his apostlis & alle his martirs & trewe men in þis world, & proue eche
> kyng in cristendom forsworn & no kyng; but certis god techiþ in his lawe þat
> o trewe man, as danuel dede, schal conuyete two false prestis...[28]

> {bring many false witnesses and notaries in his absence, who yet in his
> presence speak no word, and they feign to adhere to this false law, by which
> if 3 or 4 false witnesses hired for money say such a thing against a true man,
> then he him-self shall not be heard, even though he might be able to prove the
> contrary on the strength of two or three hundred witnesses. By this manner
> of proceeding these false men effectively declare that Christ was lawfully put
> to death, and Susanna the same, for it was by such witnesses that they were
> condemned. But Christian theology teaches the contrary. Moreover, by this
> falsified law they may "prove" to be heretics whoever they wish; yea, Christ
> and all his apostles, his martyrs and all faithful persons in this world, and
> prove as well each king in Christendem foresworn and no king. Yet it is
> certain that God teaches in his law that one faithful person shall be able, as
> Daniel did, to convert two false priests....}

That trial proceedings such as are suggested here were common enough

---

[27] Hudson, *Two Wycliffite Texts*, 35. Thorpe's association of Susanna with this strategy
may owe to the lengthy praise of her in this regard by St. Ambrose, who sees her silence as
an active, rather than a passive virtue: "there is also an active silence, such as Susanna's was,
who did more by keeping silence than if she had spoken" (*De officiis ministrorum* 1.39), and
further, "Susanna was silent in danger, and thought the loss of modesty worse than the loss
of life. She did not accept that her safety should be preserved at the cost of her chastity.
To God alone she spoke, to whom she could speak out in true modesty. She avoided looking
on the face of men" (1.18.68).

[28] Matthew, 74-5.

between 1396-1420 is a matter abundantly attested in the records. But the comparison of the situation of the accused with both Christ and Susanna as falsely accused innocents is also typical of the self-conscious biblicism of Wycliffite self-defence[29]; it is not surprising that the ME poet has Susanna plead for God's forgiveness for her false accusers (1. 241) in evident adumbration of the biblical source. Typically Wycliffite also is the characterization of the two lecherous elders as "priests" rather than judges or even "false prophets" -- "priests" is the term used by the ME poet of the *Pistel of Swete Susan* exclusively after the third stanza.[30]

The text commonly referred to as "Wycliffe's Apology" also makes central use of the Susanna story in attacking contemporary examples of unjust judgment against the innocent. Here the sources include, beside key biblical texts on the sin of bearing or upholding false witness -- centrally, of course, the decalogue itself (Ex. 20:16; cf. Ex. 23:1-3) -- explicit reference to the commentary upon Dan. 13 of Ambrose, and implicit reference to Aquinas' discussion of the unjust use of evidence and the mutual sin of false witness -- texts from the *Summa Theologica* to which Wyclif had been indebted in his *De domino civilo* and *De domino divino.* Susanna accordingly makes her appearance in "Wycliffe's Apology" somewhat in the shadow of an agent of the "God who judges," her deliverer Daniel:

> Daniel seith thus: Sey 3e sonis of Israel folis, noiþer knowing nor deming þing þat is verrey, turniþ a3en to þe dome, and I schal deme hem wisely, for þei han seid fals witnes a3enis her. In wilk is to be notid wel, þat fals dome may be reuokid, and þo iugis not excusid, bi þer witnes, but more gilty for wickid consent; and in þis þei consent, þat þei werk wickidly; for þe man schal not vndir go þe peyn, befor þat þe iuge 3eft þe dome; nor it helpiþ not to sey þat he schal be excusid bi þis, þat God seiþ, þat ilk work schal stond in þe mouþ of two or of þre, for þat may not implye þat al þing is soþe for þey sey it, but it is seid for þis, þat no man schal be condempnid bi on seying witnes a3en him, os þe scripture declariþ itsilf.[31]

> {Daniel says this: "Look you who are fools among the sons of Israel, able neither to recognize nor to judge things in such a way as to get at the truth, turn again to the courtroom and I shall judge them wisely, for in fact they have uttered false witness against her." On the strength of this scripture it is to be noted that a false judgment may be revoked and the [offending] judges not excused of their taking such witness, but held all the more guilty for wicked consent [in letting it stand]. For in consenting [to perjury] they act

---

[29] The only other common parallel drawn by Wycliffite apologists is with Moses. See, e.g., *An Apology for Lollard Doctrine*, ed. J.H. Todd (London: Camden Society, 1842), 21. Here, in "Wycliffe's Apology," when the example of Jesus not cursing his tormentors is adduced: "Also be ensaumple of Moyses, wan þe peple synnid in to God ... wan þei greuid him he þolid, and 3aue the cause to God."

[30] In line 39 they are "juges"; in line 40 "demers."

[31] Todd, 63.

wickedly, since the accused ought not to be permitted to suffer punishment before the judge has given [a proper] judgment. Nor does it help [abrogate their judicial culpability] to claim that it is sufficient excuse that God has said that each decision shall be determined on the basis of two or three witnesses, since that [provision] was not intended to imply that everything [two or three witnesses] say is true just because they say it. Rather, [that law] is given for this purpose, that no one should be condemned by merely one person giving witness against him, as the Scripture itself makes plain.}

So accusers ought to be wary that they do not assert they know something to be true which is not, for at the Last Judgment then "shall God condemn them out of their own mouth, when they have asserted things which may not be proven, when or where it was done, as Daniel did [in the case of] the priests" (66). Here and throughout the Wycliffite text is making indirect use (via Wyclif's Latin works) of Thomas Aquinas on the matter of injustice on the part of witnesses. For Aquinas himself two biblical stories highlight this problem. Susanna is one of them, but in this discussion she is invoked by Thomas only via another intermediary discussion, that of Chrysostom in his homily on Susanna and Joseph.[32] The other narrative that comes to his mind is from the annals of the reign of Ahab -- King Ahab that is, not the false prophet of that name from Jer. 29 associated by both Jewish and Christian tradition with one of the two lecherous elders. The parallel, however, will serve: Thomas writes: "certainty is not secured by the evidence of two witnesses, as we learn from Kings: Naboth was falsely condemned on the word of two witnesses. The evidence of two or three witnesses, therefore, does not suffice."[33] This leads Aquinas into a discussion of how to deal with disagreement among witnesses. He concludes

> that evidence does not establish infallible certainty but only probability, from which it follows that anything that upsets the balance of probability makes the evidence valueless. Now a person's evidence becomes less likely to be reliable on various grounds: sometimes because there is some fault -- as in the

---

[32] It is noteworthy that Thomas' teacher Albertus Magnus makes heavy use in his commentary on Daniel of Maimonides. See his *Commentarius in librum Danielis prophetae*, Opera Omnia, 8 (Lyons: Aschendorff, 1651), 606-59. In the sermon of Chrysostom Thomas has in mind Chrysostom is interested primarily in Susanna's chastity, in which she "stood as a lamb between two wolves... with no one to help her but God alone." Hence she has become "a glorious example to women of all times. Susanna endured a severe fight, more severe than that of Joseph. He, a man, contended with one woman; but Susanna, a woman, had to contend with two men, and was a spectacle to men and to angels. The slander against her fidelity to her marriage-vow, the fear of death, her condemnation by all the people, the abhorrence of her husband and relations, the tears of her servants, the grief of all her household -- she foresaw all this, and yet nothing could shake her fortitude" (trans. in B. Metzger, *An Introduction to the Apocrypha* (New York: Oxford University Press, 1957), 112. Cf. Chrysostom, Homily no. 1, PG 57.16. See also Ambrose, *De Spiritu Sancto* 3.6.39-43.

[33] Aquinas, *Summa Theologica* 2a2ae, 70.1.

case of betrayal of the faith...[34]

These points are quite expressly mirrored in the Wycliffite "Apology" (61-2) as also is Aquinas' declaration (in respect of Ex. 20:16 and Prov. 19:5, 9) that self-conscious provision of false evidence (perjury) is always a mortal sin ("Apology," 60); predictably, in the Wycliffite texts these arguments are much expanded upon rhetorically. The emphasis in the *Pistel of Swete Susan* on the matter of cross-examination largely follows the Vulgate -- though it is noteworthy that the Vulgate's extensive praise of Daniel's method did not occasion more development in the ME poem in this regard. In view of the fact that the two lecherous "priests" in the ME poem twice refer to the "lorer" (laurel) tree under which they proposition Susanna, it is also remarkable that neither, when given opportunity to name the tree under which she was said by them to have committed her deed of impurity, could remember this. Indeed, the poet makes them do no better than ineffectively mimic the Greek (or Aramaic) puns of the original story -- puns which precisely link their fate with their lie -- by a contrived English assonance ("cyne" and "prine").[35] One wonders if the "laurel" under which Susanna is found in the ME poem is not in fact meant, in a kind of dramatic irony, to conjure up the crown of victory reserved for the faithful, hence bound to go unnoticed by such obvious "losers" (cf. l. 161) as the false priests.[36]

It seems that these ancillary texts further situate our ME *Pistel of Swete Susan* securely in the context of Wycliffite concerns about oppression by false witness and the unjust use of evidence. The betrayal of an innocent "trewe" person, a very model of fidelity both to her marriage vows and to the law of God, betrayal by the very people one expects by vocation to uphold these laws -- indeed who sit, as the Wycliffite writers used to say, in the "chair of Moses" -- this was to them an all too familiar predicament. The author of the *Pistel of Swete Susan* clearly shares the almost universal contempt for such *traducteurs* expressed by Wycliffite apologists as well as by Aquinas. They agree, too, with Aquinas in his commentary on Jeremiah 23:14, that "a sin committed by a person with religious vocation may be more serious than a sin of the same species committed by lay persons."[37] The character of the ME Susanna as an attack on essentially apostate ecclesiasts, with an implicit prophecy of their ultimate undoing, is, in pious Wycliffite writings, a recurrent polemical feature; the virtue of Daniel's effective deliverance of the betrayed innocent is that it

---

[34] *Summa Theologica* 2a2ae, 70.3.

[35] Charles, 2.642; Metzger, 110-11; cf. Hastings, 4.632, who finds equally effective puns in Aramaic. The assumption of biblical scholars is that no such puns would have been possible in biblical Hebrew.

[36] Cf. St. Paul, 1 Cor. 9:24-25; 2 Tim. 2:5 and commentaries by Augustine and Lyra especially.

[37] *Summa Theologica* 2a2ae, 186.10. This is a nearly ubiquitous theme in Fitzralph, William of St. Amours and various anti-fraternal polemicists as well.

shows the problem experienced by persons such as Susanna is not with the "Law of Moses" in which she also has been instructed, but rather with its perversion by unjust "ministers of the Law" who abuse it for their own foul purposes. Deliverance still comes, as in the case of the narrative about the woman taken in adultery in the Gospel for the same day, by a just application of the Law's own standard of justice by a "trewe man." Consistently, on the view expressed in the Wycliffite sermon on the Gospel, even the adulterous woman's problem seems in some sense less with the Law of God than with the finagling laws of men which encumber it:

> Here men seien þat Goddis lawe is just, boþe þe olde lawe and þe newe, but of mannis lawe þei seien not so, but supposen þat it be often unjust. And 3it þes þat shulden holde Goddis lawe, synnen ofte in uss of it. But þis we taken as bileve, þat Goddis lawe is ever good, and men synnen not in uss of it, but 3if þer synne bifore be cause. And herfore justisis of ech lawe shulden be ri3twis and clene of liif; for God mut reule men of þe lawe, how þei shulen juge in ech caas.[38]

> {Here men may legitimately say that the Law of God itself is just, both the Old Law and the New. Yet of human laws they are not able to say so, but must suppose them often to be unjust. And yet it remains the case that those who should maintain the Law of God sin often in their application of it. But this we take on faith, that the Law of God in itself is good in all respects, and men do not sin in implementing it unless their own state of sin beforehand is the cause [of their miscreance]. Accordingly justices of each law [God's law and human law] should be righteous and clean-living, for God must rule men of the law [guiding them] how they should judge in each case.}

This is Wyclif's argument in his *De domino civilo* and *De domino divino* in a nutshell. Indeed, refusal of the distinction between person and office as a species of false *distinctio* came to be regarded by his opponents as one of his chief heresies.

The beautiful elaboration of the garden setting, the poet's lush description like a tapestry finely woven, ought not in the case of this poem to be taken as warrant for reading it only -- or perhaps we should say "merely" -- allegorically. To be sure, for the early Christian church the genre of the Susanna text was always an uncertain matter. Theodotion treated it as history; Jerome, with "some hesitation," includes it under prophecy. After Hippolytus (Bishop of Rome ca. 230 A.D.) allegory predominated in Christian commentary and artistic treatment: Susanna was the *sponsa* or faithful bride, the Church; Joachim, her *sponsus*, Christ, and the garden the *b'rith* of the saints and their fruitfulness *dor le dor*. Babylon stood for the world and the two elders were

---

[38] Hudson, *English Wycliffite Sermons*, 126-7.

types of those who persecute the faithful, both Jewish and Gentile.[39] This is the sort of parallel allegorizing (cf. the Song of Songs) that appealed to Origen in his *Stromata* (10), which still occurs in Rabanus Maurus and is developed through much of Renaissance and even into 19th century Catholic homiletical treatments of the text. It is this tradition which attaches itself to several of the Latin medieval poems of Susanna, and which led Alfred Kellogg to associate it along with the Song of Songs as a parodic backdrop for the garden of love in Chaucer's Merchant's Tale.[40] But not here. The Wycliffites, like Lyra before them, were deeply committed to the *sensus literalis*, and their exegesis is overwhelmingly historical, with <u>moralite</u> drawn upon it straightforwardly. Susanna in the *Pistel of Swete Susan* is therefore not to be imagined as an inverted Eve or immaculate redeemed bride, the raptured Church without spot and wrinkle. Nor is it necessary to make of Daniel an analogue for the Holy Spirit[41] or a second Christ figure in order for them, as they imagine, to read the poem in the spirit in which it was written. The *Pistel of Swete Susan* is meant to be an historical poem by genre, bearing a clear moral for all times. This moral is that the best of men and women, true husbands, wives and would-be keepers of the Law of God, can be victimized by unscrupulous self-servers, even those who may cast themselves as upholders of the Law of God. Against such, for righteous Wycliffite Christian as for righteous Jew, there is but one course of defence -- an obedient trust in and knowledge of the Law both deeper and more exacting than that of those who persecute the faithful. Such knowledge may or may not save its knower from a stony demise, but eternally

> Hose leeveth on that Lord, thar him not lees, That thus his servaunt saved that schold ha be schent In sete.

> [Whoever believes in the Lord need not suffer perdition, For this is the God who saved his servant, who otherwise would have been destroyed On the spot.]

The sweteness in Susan's "epistle," savored in this 14th- century English encomium, is thus a familiar sweetness (Ps. 119:103-4), and palatable still to a diversity of tongues and tastes.

---

[39] Charles, 640ff; cf. Origen, *Stromata* 10; Rabanus Maurus, *De universu*, ed. Migne, PL 112.

[40] Kellogg, op. cit.

[41] Ambrose says that as a result of her prayer the Holy Spirit was sent to Susanna; Daniel in turn was enabled by the same Holy Spirit to discover "that lustful adultery, that fraudulent lie." *De Spiritu Sancto* 3.6.41,43.

Sexual Slander and the Politics of the Erotic in Garter's *Susanna*

M. Lindsay Kaplan
Georgetown University

This chapter explores the cultural work one version of the Susanna story performed in Elizabethan England. The general popularity of this tale in Christian culture suggests not only its inherent attractiveness but also a certain plasticity: its elements can be shaped to serve different religious, social, and aesthetic ends. The apocryphal account of Susanna appeared in a variety of forms in Renaissance England: popular wall pictures, ballads and drama. Tessa Watt notes in her book *Cheap Print and Popular Piety* that Susanna was one of the four most popular subjects of biblical wall paintings which "illustrate the fusion of various cultural strands: the Protestant impetus for popularization of the Scriptures, the iconophobic tendency to avoid the more sacred figures of Christianity and the traditional demand for narrative pictures" (203). However, here the erotic component of this story seems to provide the basis of its appeal, since the representations seem to have served an entertaining rather than a didactic purpose (209). Similarly, with regard to ballad versions, Watt suggests that their real interest "lay in the image of naked Susanna washing herself in the orchard, an object of fantasy which probably titillated the viewers of Renaissance paintings on the theme just as much as it did the wicked elders whose lechery was supposedly condemned" (119).[1]

The dramatic representation of the story, Thomas Garter's *Comedy of the Most Virtuous and Godly Susanna*, combines strands of the sacred and the profane. Murray Roston has noted in his discussion of the play, that part of its attraction lies in its biblical provenance:

> The books of the Apocrypha were still holy, to be treated with deference and respect, but their holiness was many degrees below that of the canonical books, and hence the dramatist felt a greater freedom in handling his material.

---

[1] See Joyce Sexton for a bibliography of Susanna stories in medieval and Renaissance literature (96, note 4).

... The haloes have been removed, and the audience can see the biblical
characters as human beings rather than as demi-gods. This change forms part
of the new identification with biblical characters which Protestantism and,
particularly, the translation of the Bible into the vernacular had produced. (91)

However, if the "concern with theodicy...remained to the fore as the central
message of the Renaissance scriptural plays" the influence of classical sources
also made itself felt (Roston 87). Roston astutely notes Garter's indebtedness
to pagan, particularly Ovidian eroticism, in the playwright's allusions to the
story of Diana and Actaeon and various quotations from Ovid and Virgil.

In spite of these gestures, the play resists exploiting the sexual potential
of its subject by following the apocryphal version (at least in this regard) and
keeping Susanna fully clothed. This is in part a practical choice; nudity would
not have been tolerated on the stage even in a less "godly" play and the English
Renaissance convention of an all-male cast of actors would have posed
difficulties in presenting the spectacle of Susanna bathing.[2]

However, the theater was certainly capable of creating erotic effects when
desired, either in the bawdy innuendo of pun and stage business or in the more
sophisticated seductions of representation with which Stephen Greenblatt
characterizes the Renaissance stage (88-93). If Garter chose not to emphasize
these aspects of the story, what issues did he emphasize and why?

A consideration of how Garter frames and develops the apocryphal
material will help answer these questions. The play opens, after a short
summarizing prologue, with Satan speculating how he can corrupt Susanna, the
only truly virtuous person living in Babylon. Having failed to incite her to
many of the deadly sins, he now "With filthy lustes of fleshly men, meaneth her
to assayle,/ And such they be shall her intise, to do that pleasant deede,/ As
shall preuayle I tell you true, by force or else by meede" (ll. 176-8). While he
employs Voluptas and Sensualitas, the personified qualities representing the two
elders, his chief assistant in this task is not some other representation of lust,
but his son, Ill Report. He is less interested in Susanna's response to the
concupiscent elders than in her humiliation. That is, though Satan seems
initially more interested in her internal state of sin or innocence, Ill Report shifts
the emphasis to discrediting her regardless of her culpability. He muses on the
success of his plot:

> And when that they haue got their wils, and so haue wrought her shame,
> My selfe will blow the leaden Trumpe of cruell slanderous fame,
> Lo thus my Dad I please I trow, and thus my nature showe,
> Thus shall ech man my power and might in euery corner blow,
> And say that though the Deuill himselfe, could not tempt Susans grace
> The wit of Mayster Ill Report hath her and it defaste. (ll. 179-84)

---

[2] However, for a suggestive argument to the contrary on the erotic potential of
transvestite actors, see Stallybrass.

His boast suggests that the devil might fail in tempting Susanna to commit a sin; however, his slander will succeed in shaming her even if she is innocent.[3]

The action of the play thus centers around establishing the circumstances which will enable Susanna's slander. While the elders' lust is a primary factor in the plan, their longings for her do not create an erotic mood. As often as not, they are the dupes of Ill Report's con games and tricks, objects of audience mockery rather than identification. While their raptures over Susanna verge on the Ovidian at times, as Roston points out (88-90), they also lapse into crude innuendo; as Sensualitas remarks (and we can almost feel the elbow-nudge in our ribs), "By God I would spende my best cote to fish within her poole" (427)! However, even in the midst of their foolish hungerings, the elders also express concern over their reputations:

> But we are counted Elders here, and doe the people guide,
> And [w]hat we doe must secrete be, least that we be espide,
> For God, or for his threatninges, I passe it not a straw,
> But for myne honour in this world, is it I stand in aw. (431-4)

Anxious as they are about their reputations, they are also aware of Susanna's renowned virtuousness and fear that in a conflict with her, she might be believed over them. They propose a plan to protect their own credit while advancing their lecherous designs:

> And therefore if we could by crafte, some slaunder on her rayse,
> It might helpe well our credite when, we seeke our lust to please.

While attending both to the sensuous and slanderous aspects of his material, Garter clearly gives primacy to defamation over debauchery.

In focusing on issues of honor and infamy, Garter taps into one of the prominent anxieties of the Renaissance period. Reputation was of paramount concern among rich and poor, titled and common, and male and female in early modern England, as court records and other written evidence of the period attests. The sixteenth century in England witnessed a rapid increase and expansion of litigation over defamation in both ecclesiastical and secular courts. As J. A. Sharpe argues, "the rise in defamation suits is one of the most striking developments in the business of the courts during this period" (4). While I am unable to explore slander's full complexity in one essay, I would nevertheless like to focus on an important aspect of this phenomenon that related to the concerns of Garter's play.

Gender affected both the content of and redress for defamation, due, to a large extent, to differences in the way reputation was constructed. As Susan Amussen observes:

---

[3] Sexton notes that this notion of slander being more powerful than the devil is also evident in Gower's *Mirour de l'Omme* (44).

> ...defamation cases suggest that 'honesty' had one meaning for women and
> another for men. Women's honesty was determined and judged by their
> sexual behavior; men's honesty was judged in a wide variety of contexts with
> their neighbours, and bore a closer relation to our notion of honesty as
> 'truthful'. Reputation was a gendered concept in early modern England. (104)

Male reputation was based on class status, authority in the community and
household (including control over his wife's sexuality), financial standing and
religious practice. Men could sue either for damages in the common law courts
for slanders which resulted in financial loss, or for a public apology in
ecclesiastical courts for false accusations of "spiritual" crimes such as
blasphemy, perjury or fornication. On the other hand, female reputation was
based primarily on her sexual behavior. Except in rare cases, she could not sue
for damages in the common law courts. The primary epithet against which
women litigate in the ecclesiastical courts is that of "whore"; charges of adultery
and fornication run a close second (Sharpe 10).

J. A. Sharpe speculates that the gendered nature of defamation reflects the
differences in social roles for men and women.

> ...it is difficult not to see the wider types of defamation against which men
> litigated as a consequence of their more varied involvement in the affairs of
> the world. Women... were allowed free access to everyday activities, but
> their role within them was limited. The rarity with which they were slandered
> as perjurers, cheats, and usurers, for example, suggests that they were not
> allowed to participate very fully in business or legal matters. (29)

But this is only a partial explanation, since it does not account for the fact that
female reputation is based on her sexual behavior. In *The Creation of
Patriarchy*, Gerda Lerner notes that, unlike a man's reputation, a woman's has
been determined historically by her sexual behavior: "We shall encounter the
principle that a man's class status is determined by his economic relations and
a woman's by her sexual relations in a number of...instances in this period
[approximately 1750 B.C.E. to the 8th c. B.C.E.] of the formation of class
society. It is a principle which has remained valid for thousands of years" (106-
7).

The definition of female reputation in terms of her sexual behavior
manifests itself in a misogynist strand of the Christian tradition with the claim
that women are inherently lustful. In his recent book *Carnal Israel*, Daniel
Boyarin explores the larger Hellenistic context of this perspective, which
condemns the corporeal and the sexual, often associated with the female body.
These ideas not only influence later conceptions of gender, but help form the
basis of and supply the authority for debates about women in the English
Renaissance (Henderson and McManus 8).

This conception of women in terms of their sexuality has a material basis
as well; the Renaissance English husband not only took control over his wife's
property upon marriage, he also acquired property in her body. The children

she produced belonged to him and the continuity of the family (for middling and upper classes) depended on the creation of a legitimate male heir to carry on its name and maintain control over its financial holdings. Anxiety about female promiscuity fixates on the possibility that the wife's children might not be her husband's, and that his property will be transmitted to another man's son. The assertion of an independent female sexuality also belies the fiction that her husband owns her body or the children she gives birth to by demonstrating that her sexual choices are beyond his control.

Thus, sexual slander, while perceived as a problem by its victims, nevertheless performed a valuable patriarchal function. The threat of public humiliation and rejection certainly served as a deterrent both for victims of slander as well as chaste and promiscuous by-standers. The fact that women could not sue at the common law for damages in cases of sexual slander is a measure of the lesser status in which defamations against females were held. Even in cases where women could show damages for sexual slander, the common law courts were reluctant to provide redress for a "spiritual offense" - - an uncharacteristic show of self-restraint in relation to the jurisdiction of the ecclesiastical courts (Baker and Milsom 627-8).

Nevertheless, this negative characterization of female sexuality did not go unchallenged in the early modern period. In the pamphlet wars over gender in Renaissance England both male and female writers challenged the association of women with unbridled sexuality. In Edward Gosynhill's *Mulierum Paean*, probably published in 1542, Susanna appears at the end of a long description of heroines from Hebrew, Christian and classical traditions:

That one remembred conclude I shall
The hystory I meane of good Susan
Falsely accused by the man.

Attempt she was of rybaldes two
With them to haue dealed, she nolde consent
They her accused, and sayde she had ado
With a yonge man, and shulde be brent
God knowe the woman innocent
And caused the infant Danyell
To speak to the people and the treuth tell.

A babe to speke was a straunge maruell
The people assembled on euery syde
The tales bothe varyed that they did tell
Wherby it was knowen the rybaldes lyde
The woman saued and the treuth tryde
Her false accusars by comen assent
To dye forthwith had iust iudgement. (Eii v-Eiii r)

She is held up as the chaste model who vindicates the virtue of women and refocuses attention on the behavior of the lascivious elders (Henderson & McManus 168).

Garter's representation of Susanna could therefore function as an everywoman, a defender of her gender, especially given the morality play flavor of the drama with its personified sins and characteristic vice figure in the person of Ill Report. While she may have signified as this general type, she nevertheless seems to be marked in the play as an exemplary figure. Her outstanding reputation for virtue, her unwavering faith in God and her trial by a devilish adversary connect her story with another biblical trial, that of Job. Job is described at the outset of the biblical narrative thus:[4]

> There was a man in the land of 'Vz, whose name was Iob, and this man was an vpright and iuste man, one that feared God, & eschewed euil. (1:1)

Later, when Satan, or the adversary, meets with God, the latter describes Job in almost identical terms:

> Hast thou not considered my seruant Iob, how none is like him in earth, an vpright and iust man, one that feareth God, and escheweth euil? (1:8)

Susanna is similarly described by the devil:

> Yet there is one in Babilon,
> That neuer had not peere,
> She serueth God and on him sets,
> Her study and her care. (ll. 78-81)

and by Ill Report:

> There is in all this Babilon, but one that he doth spye,
> That feareth God, and eke my Dad in all his workes defye. (ll. 151-2)

The Devil aims to overthrow those who fear God, and Susanna seems to be the one person who fits this description in Babylon. The successful humiliation of Susanna would be seen as a triumph over God, as she is his foremost adherent. The Devil's plan is ultimately a challenge to God:

> And let us see if God with all his myght,
> Can defende this soule from our auncient spyght. (ll. 115-16)

The threat of sexual slander to Susanna promises to have serious theological consequences.

---

[4] Citations are from the Geneva Bible.

The religious significance of the devil's trial of Susanna is hinted at in the representation of her immediate adversaries. Voluptas and Sensualitas' apparel suggests their connection with Catholicism and the Church of Rome. In a humorous exchange in which he complains of the elders informality towards him, Ill Report draws attention to their clothes:

> What playne <u>Ill Report</u>, no mayster at all,
> in fayth for all your bloody gowne, I will rap you on the scall. (ll. 528-9)

After Daniel has accused the elders of slandering the innocent Susanna, Ill Report again draws attention to their attire, with a reference to the custom of the hangman taking ownership of the clothes of his victim.[5]

> Come on you knaue, thou bawdy wretch, I hope to have thy cote,
> And for exchaunge thereof thou shalt be strangled in a rope.
> Mary syr a bloody gowne vpon my back, will make me look a hye.
> And then that I am Ill Report, no worldly man can spye. (ll. 1140-3)

The "bloody gownes" are almost certainly a reference to red coats worn by cardinals in the Roman Catholic Church. Ben Jonson's play *The Alchemist* satirizes the Protestant revulsion for Catholicism precisely in this context when Tribulation argues that the reformers must stand "Against the menstrous cloth, and ragg of <u>Rome</u>[!]" (III.i.33). Garter extends this view to the common Puritan association of Catholicism with the Antichrist in the opening passages of the play, where Ill Report lists those who "weare bloody gownes" (174) among the souls the devil has obtained by means of gold.[6]

The exemplary virtuousness of Susanna, her special relationship to God and the attacks on her reputation by veiled representatives of Catholicism, all suggest that she might be a figure for England's latter day chaste defender of the Faith, Queen Elizabeth. As monarch, Elizabeth was also supreme governor of the Church of England, thus representing the head of the English Reform movement (Haigh 30). This is a role that Elizabeth herself embraced; as Christopher Haigh points out, "In the collection of private devotions she composed about 1579, Queen Elizabeth presented herself as God's instrument for the restoration of the Gospel, as mother of he Church in England, and as protectress of religious refugees" (27). She was also publicly identified with this role, often in the context of examples set by women holding positions of authority in Hebrew Scripture. As the Protestant Duchess of Suffolk commented, "If the Israelites might joy in their Deborah, how much more we

---

[5] See note to IV.ii.41-5, p. 102, Arden *Measure for Measure*.

[6] It should also be noted in this context, and given the names of the elders, that the Catholic church was also characterized by Protestants as a sink of depravity. Luther's allegations of sexual perversions in the Church, which he saw as resulting from the generally impossible dictate of celibacy, are particularly eloquent on this subject (Witte).

English in our Elizabeth" (quoted in Haigh 28). In the entertainment presented to the queen in Norwich on her royal progress of 1578, Elizabeth was, in one poem, again likened to Deborah, in addition to Judith and Esther. This poem was composed by a Bernard Garter, an anti-catholic minor poet, who may have been the playwright's brother or the playwright himself (Garter v-vi); both the play and the text of the entertainment were published in 1578. In the drama, Susanna herself is loosely linked with queenship when she is being sentenced to death by the judge of her trial:

> Thou seest here before thy face, how playne thy fault is seene,
> For as I doe, I must needes doe, although thou were a Queene. (1053-4)

An even more striking connection appears before the closing speech is read by the speaker of the Prologue, when the biblical characters of the play anachronistically offer prayers for Elizabeth, her counselors and the Parliament.

What does the story of Susanna have to do with the life of the Virgin Queen of England? It seems highly improbable that a woman who never married or bore children could be linked with a figure accused of adultery. However, given the earlier discussion of the sexual basis of the formulation of women's reputations, it is not surprising that Elizabeth repeatedly found herself the victim of sexual slander. Rumors alleging sexual misconduct in Elizabeth's private life circulated repeatedly throughout her reign, revealing that even the queen was not protected from her gender. As a young single woman and ruler, she was actively sought as a wife by foreign and domestic suitors alike. Her affection for Robert Dudley early in her reign caused such a flurry of scandal in England and on the Continent that the representative for one her wooers felt it necessary to inquire if Elizabeth were still a virgin (Neale 79-83). Outside of court, stories circulated to the effect that she had borne Dudley an illegitimate child. Slanders regarding the queen and Dudley, who later became the earl of Leicester, returned in the 1560s, 80s and 90s, long after the end of her child-bearing years and the Earl's death (Samaha 69).

However, Elizabeth was also susceptible to slanderous imputations with regard to her public status. As a female ruler, she -- like Mary Tudor and Mary, Queen of Scots -- contradicted conventional wisdom which held that women could not be superior to men. Their general weakness and inferiority were cited by authors of treatises against queenship; one serious concern voiced was that once freed from male control, female lust would know no bounds.[7] John Knox articulated this sentiment in his anti-Catholic attack on Mary Tudor's reign; however, he refused to retract his opinion on Elizabeth's succession:

---

[7] It is worth noting that a common slang word for whore in this period was the term "queane"; no such analogous pejorative term exists for promiscuous males, rulers or otherwise. For overviews of the queenship debates, see Scalingi and Jordan; see also Levin for an account of the anxiety of Elizabeth's subjects in being ruled by a woman.

Wold to God the examples were not so manifest, to the further declaration of the imperfections of women, of her naturall weaknes, and inordinat appetites. I might adduce histories, prouing some women to haue died for sodein ioy, some for vnpaciencie to haue murthered themselues, some to haue burned with such inordinat lust, that for the quenching of the same, they haue betrayed to strangiers their countrie and citie. (14)

Christopher Goodman offered a similar description of Mary's rule in his attack on the passivity of her subjects:

Yet are you willingly become, as it were, bondemen to the lustes of a most impotent and vnbrydled women: a woman begotten in adultrie a bastarde by birthe, contrary to the worde of God a[n]d your owne lawes. (97)

Mary's status as a queen was called into question not only by allegations of her own sexual impropriety, but also that of her parents. Henry's marriage to Mary's mother, Katherine of Aaragon, was dissolved and Mary's birth declared illegitimate when Henry sought a new marriage he hoped would provide him with a male heir.

The nature of Elizabeth's own lineage and accession to the throne also generated slander during her rule, thus linking her more directly with Susanna's adultery charge. The Catholic Church challenged the validity of Henry VIII's divorce from Katherine of Aaragon and rejected the legitimacy of his subsequent marriage with Anne Boleyn, Elizabeth's mother. Catholics viewed this union as an adulterous one and considered Elizabeth a bastard. Henry added fuel to this fire three years after his marriage to Anne when he charged her with adultery, incest, and treason and had her executed and Elizabeth declared illegitimate. In establishing the second act of succession, Henry removed the injunction against slanders of Anne and Elizabeth he had legislated earlier in the wake of criticisms over his divorce from Katherine; he, in effect, confirmed and legalized Catholic opinion in pardoning slanders against his second wife and her daughter:

...the kings most roiall maiestie, most generouslie considering, that diuers and manie of his most louing and obedient subiects now latelie after the beginning of the present parlement, haue spoken,...[etc.] against the said vnlawfull mariage, solemnized betweene his highnesse and the said ladie Anne, and to the preiudice, slander disturbance and derogation therof, but also to the perill slander and disherison of the ladie Elizabeth the kings daughter illegitimat borne vnder the same mariage, and to the let disturbance and interruption of the said ladie Elizabeth to the title of the crowne:........ Which words, dooings, etc albeit they proceeded of not malice, but vpon true and iust grounds, ...yet neuerthelesse the kings said subiects might heereafter happen to be impeached, troubled, and vexed for such their words, dooings, acts, etc.......The kings highnesse therefore of his most bountifull mercie and benignitie is pleased and contented that it be enacted...that all and singular his louing subiects, which haue spoken,...etc against [the marriage, Anne or Eliz],

or to anie of their slanders, perils or disherison:...shall be freelie and cleerelie
pardoned, discharged, and released by authoritie of this act, of all those and
such treasons and misprisions of treasons aboue mentioned. (28 HVIII c.7)

These charges against Elizabeth and Anne continued to surface well into her
reign. Catholic propaganda alluding to Elizabeth's adulterous origins and
linking them with her own alleged promiscuity circulated with increasing
frequency and virulence as the sixteenth century wore on.

Given the volume and variety of sexual slander experienced by Elizabeth,
it might be tempting to read Garter's play as straightforward defense of her
virtue, and her queenly authority in general, against her attackers. However,
a closer look at the denouement of the action suggests certain limitations in the
dramatist's support of his queen's status.

When the two elders proposition Susanna in the garden, she calls on God
for help, but her tormenters, not she -- in contrast to the apocryphal narrative -
- cry for help. Of the two servants who respond to the call, one is named True
Report; he assures his companion Seruus that their mistress is indeed innocent
and correctly predicts the downfall of the elders before Daniel even appears.
The addition of True Report to the action significantly lessens Daniel's role,
since we are assured that right will prevail. His presence would also seem to
offer, in the eyes of the audience, almost superfluous support for Susanna. His
report does not change the action of the play -- Daniel is still needed to prove
her innocence.   Additionally, the audience already knows that Susanna is
innocent, having witnessed the plots laid by the devil, Ill Report and the elders
in contrast to her virtuous behavior. Though this advocacy for Susanna clearly
determines her innocence, the effect of the entire scene works to cancel her
agency and independence.[8]

During the trial scene, a generic judge, Iudex, presides over the
preliminary questioning and sentencing; Susanna's husband is conspicuously
absent. When the judge pronounces Susanna's death sentence, Daniel speaks
out in her behalf, echoing the language of the apocryphal narrative. When
Susanna insisted on her own innocence in the trial, she is not believed; however
when Daniel speaks out, before he has even offered any evidence in support of
his claims, he is immediately believed by the judge and authorized by him to
retry the case:

> Mary chylde with all my hart, we will retourne vs soone, And also what thou
> thinkest meete, it shall straight way be done, And synce that God by thee have

---

[8] Sexton sees Susanna's passivity here as a typical result of the effects of slander: "...it
is because [Garter is] accentuating the moral seriousness of slander and the meaning of
defamation that [the] accused [woman is] passive and helpless in these scenes.... [Susanna
behaves] in accordance with the traditional sense that the victim of detraction is helpless"
(45).

giuen, a warning to vs all, come sit with vs in iudgement seate, least we
agayne y should fall. (1075-8)

However, once Daniel questions the elders and proves their guilt, he disappears
entirely from the play. When the judge asks him to give sentence, Daniel
refuses and exits the stage, leaving Ill Report to preside over the execution of
the guilty parties.

These shifts in the story, though subtle, are, I think significant. The
presentation of Daniel would seem simultaneously to increase and diminish his
importance in the play. Closer inspection, however reveals that his authority
is only increased vis à vis Susanna. While his limited presence in the play
preserves Susanna's role as the central character, the superiority of his
credibility subordinates her to this ephemeral prophet.

If Daniel has a small part, it is nevertheless a crucial one because it
demonstrates her complete passivity and dependence on a male savior. I would
also argue that the absence of her husband Ioachim during the trial scene again,
paradoxically, serves to undercut her standing. While Susanna's parents
comment on the charges brought against their daughter, Ioachim is oddly silent.
He drops out before the trial and execution of his co-judges, the elders, and
reappears only in the final lines of the play. However, his presence would
cause greater problems than the minor oddity of his absence, since he would
either have to believe the elders, which would cast unwanted aspersion on the
heroine, or believe her, which would give a credence and authority to her
speech, which the plays seems at pains to avoid.

The ambivalence of Garter's representation of Susanna resonates with the
uncertainty with which Elizabeth's supporters defended and championed her
cause. On the one hand, Protestants and other of her faithful subjects were
delighted at her accession; she was seen as restoring the true Church and
releasing England from the threat of Catholic dominance exercised during the
reign of her predecessors, Philip of Spain and Mary Tudor. On the other hand,
even her defenders were deeply uneasy at the unprecedented rule of an
unmarried female monarch. The tensions created by the intersection of deeply
held beliefs about nation, religion and the inferior position of women in the
natural order were too powerful and disjunct to be resolved. Their uneasy
coexistence in Garter's play registers his desire both to protect and defend his
queen as well as his anxiety over promoting her authority as a woman.

The representations of the Susanna story that focus on its erotic potential
serve to subordinate her not only to the elders, but also to her viewers or
readers. An objectified Susanna is deprived of agency, made subject to the will
of her pursuers and defined primarily in terms of her sexuality. Although I was
at pains at the beginning of this essay to suggest that Garter does not present
Susanna for sexual consumption in his play, she is nevertheless eroticized in the
sense that, generally, women of the early modern period, and representations
of them, were defined and understood in terms of their potential for sexual

relations with men. Garter's Susanna, like her more obviously sexualized sisters, is deprived of agency and subjected to the will of the men around her because of her gender. Ultimately, we would have to argue that, for all its allusions to religious schism, reputation and female authority, the play, like the royal subject of its allegory, cannot escape its sexual shackles.

Susanna and the Elders: Wisdom and Folly

Eleonore Stump
St. Louis University

INTRODUCTION

Daniel is traditionally taken as a paradigm of wisdom, and his uncovering of the perfidy of the elders in the story of Susanna and the Elders is generally taken as another example illustrating the same virtue.[1] Susanna, on the other hand, has generally been taken as exemplifying the traditionally praised feminine virtues of chastity and patience in suffering. These characterizations are thoroughly familiar and, at first glance, unproblematic.

What is initially puzzling, from a philosophical point of view, is the behavior of the elders. Their first foray into evil is understandable enough. Although they are men of recognized religious and social authority, officials in a community constituted by shared moral and religious values, each of them conceives a great lust for another man's wife. This is a depressingly familiar kind of evil that can surprise and afflict anybody; we may be sad, but are not surprised, to find it even in otherwise saintly individuals. But in the story of Susanna and the Elders the elders move from this common evil attitude through a series of increasingly evil acts till at the end they are attempting to use the judicial system to commit murder, in a betrayal of their community and their religion.[2]

What accounts for the elders' steep descent into evil? And how are we to understand this monstrous final evil of theirs? What state of mind could explain their actions? It is true that Susanna's screaming when they try to

---

[1] In my discussion of the story of Susanna, I am using the Theodotion version of the story, rather than the Septuagint version; and I rely on the text and notes in the *Anchor Bible vol. Daniel, Esther, and Jeremiah: The Additions*, tr. Carey A. Moore, (Doubleday and Co.; Garden City, NY: 1977). Subsequent references to this work will be given as *AB* and page numbers.

[2] See the story in *AB*, 93-107.

coerce her into relations with them makes things difficult for them. But their ways out of that difficulty are limited only by one's imagination, as the history of literature shows. They might try to pass off their actions as a test devised to see whether or not she was a virtuous wife. They might bribe their servants into providing an alibi for them, so that no one could possibly believe they were with Susanna at the time she screamed. They might use moral blackmail to keep her from giving them away -- they might threaten the lives of her parents or her husband, for example. It clearly is not necessary to try to kill Susanna in order to save themselves; and in any event, trying to kill Susanna if she would not give in to their lust was part of their original plan, even before Susanna screamed. Furthermore, their attempt on her life is not a case of their reason being swamped by passion, as it might be if, for example, they stabbed her to death in a frenzy when she rejected their initial advances. Their murderousness is premeditated, in cold blood, and it consists in the perversion of the very system of justice they are bound to uphold. Finally, what they do is made considerably worse by their role in society. As elders, they are people who have (or should have) a special understanding of religion and morality and who have a special duty to uphold both. That is one of the reasons why, as I said, their judicial attack on Susanna's life constitutes a betrayal. So, beginning with trite and small-scale evil, these elders of Israel move progressively towards the real wickedness of judicial murder. How do we account for their moral decline and their ultimate moral monstrosity?

The answer comes, I think, from a closer examination of the nature of wisdom. If we understand the nature of wisdom -- or, rather, of its opposite, folly -- then we will also be in a better position to understand the behavior and psychological state of the elders. The best account I know of wisdom, and of folly, is Thomas Aquinas's. On his account, the elders are a paradigm of folly, and their actions can be explained in terms of the relations between intellect and will laid out in his account. Furthermore, once we have understood the nature of wisdom, as Aquinas presents it, it will be clear that in the story of Susanna and the Elders the virtue of wisdom is exemplified not by Daniel, however much he was traditionally supposed to exemplify that virtue in other stories. What Daniel exemplifies here is just cleverness. In this story, wisdom is exemplified by Susanna.

AQUINAS ON INTELLECT AND WILL

Although Aquinas takes wisdom to be an intellectual virtue, he thinks that it is a function both of intellect and of will; and it is fundamental to his account that will has a significant role in the production and maintenance of belief. Because the claim that will can causally affect belief seems false to many contemporary philosophers, I will begin by briefly presenting Aquinas's views on intellect and will. Then I will explicate his view of wisdom, focusing especially on wisdom's opposed vice, folly. Finally, I will argue that Aquinas's account of wisdom and folly gives a good explanation of the common but puzzling ethical phenomenon represented by the moral monstrosity of the elders.

Contemporary philosophers tend to operate with a conception of the will as the steering wheel of the mind, neutral in its own right but able to direct other parts of the person. Aquinas's conception of the will is quite different. He takes the will to be not neutral, but a bent or inclination. The will, he says, is a hunger, an appetite, for goodness.[3] By 'goodness' here Aquinas means goodness in general, and not this or that specific good thing. Furthermore, by itself the will makes no determinations of goodness; apprehending or judging things as good is the business of the intellect. The intellect presents to the will as good certain things under certain descriptions, and the will wills them because the will is an appetite for the good, and they are apprehended as good. For this reason the intellect is said to move the will not as an efficient cause but as a final cause, because what is understood by intellect as good moves the will as an end.[4]

What the intellect determines with respect to goodness is complicated because the intellect is itself moved by other things. In the first place, the will moves the intellect as an efficient cause, for example, by commanding it directly to adopt a belief[5] or by directing it to attend to some things and to neglect others.[6] Of course, the will moves the intellect in such ways only in case the intellect represents doing so at that time as good, under some description. Every act of willing requires or is preceded by some apprehension on the part of the intellect, although not every apprehension on the part of the intellect need be preceded by an act of will.[7] In the second place, the passions -- sorrow, fury, fear, etc. -- can influence the intellect, because in the grip of a passion, such as fury, something will seem good to a person which would not seem good to her if she were calm.[8] The intellect, however, is not compelled by the passions in any way; it can resist them,[9] for example, by being aware of the passion and correcting for its effects on judgment, as one does when one leaves a letter written in anger until the next morning rather than mailing it right away.

The way the will is moved by the intellect is also complicated. The will can be moved to will rather than remaining inactive; or it can be moved to will this rather than that particular thing.[10] And in neither way is the will moved

---

[3] *ST* I-II q.10 a.1 and I q.82 a.1.

[4] *ST* I q.82 a.4.

[5] Aquinas seems to suppose that faith results from such an action of the will on the intellect. See, for example, *De veritate* where he talks of the will's commanding intellect to produce faith; *De veritate* q.14 a.3 reply, ad 2, and ad 10.

[6] See *ST* I-II q.17 a.1 and a.6.

[7] *ST* I q.82 a.4.

[8] *ST* I-II q.9 a.2.

[9] *ST* I q. 81 a.3 and I-II q.10 a.3.

[10] Cf.*ST* I-II q.9 a.1.

necessarily. Nothing in this life (apart from happiness) can move the will to will necessarily in the first way, because it is always in a person's power not to think of the thing at issue and consequently not to will it actually. In the second way, if the will is presented with an object which can be considered good under some descriptions and not good under others, then the will is not necessarily moved by that object either. So, for example, the further acquisition of money can be considered good under some descriptions -- e.g., the means of sending the children to school -- and not good under others -- e.g., wages from an immoral and disgusting job. For these reasons, no matter what earthly object (other than happiness) intellect presents to the will, the will is not constrained to move in a particular way, since it is open to the will to direct the intellect to consider that object in a variety of ways.

It should be apparent, then, that on Aquinas's account of intellect and will, the will is part of a dynamic feedback system composed of the will, the intellect, and the passions.[11] Any volition is influenced in important ways, but not caused or compelled, by previous volitions and is the result of an often complicated interaction of the intellect and the will. For that reason, although Aquinas's account of the will assigns a large role to intellect, Aquinas is not committed to seeing immoral actions simply as instances of mistakes in deliberation. In cases of incontinence, where the intellect seems to be representing something as good which the will is not willing, Aquinas would say that the intellect is in fact being moved by opposite motives to represent the thing in question as both good and not good, so that the intellect is double-minded, in some sense of that term.[12]

Finally, Aquinas not only holds that will can command intellect, but he also makes some helpful remarks about the manner in which will commands not only intellect but all the other powers of the soul under its control. The will's object is the good in general, he says, while the objects of all the other powers of the soul are particular goods; but there is order among active powers, so that the power which regards the universal end moves the powers which regard the particular ends. Consequently, the will moves the other powers of the soul with efficient causation in the way in which the general who aims at the common good of the whole army moves by his command the captains of individual companies, each of whom aims at the good of his own company.[13] In other words, Aquinas's idea is that the will works in accordance with the nature of the power of the soul it is commanding in order to help that power achieve the

---

[11] So, for example, pointing to the difficulty of extricating will and intellect from each other, Aquinas says "it happens sometimes that there is an act of the will in which something of the [preceding] act of reason remains...and, vice versa, there is [sometimes] an act of reason in which something of the [preceding] act of will remains." *ST* I-II q.17 a.1.

[12] Cf., e.g., *ST* I-II q.17 a.2 and a.5 ad 1.

[13] *ST* I-II q.9 a.1.

good it was created to achieve; will works in accordance with the design plan[14] of the faculties it governs, then, not against them.[15] Will's control over intellect, too, must respect the design plan of the intellect, which, as Aquinas puts it, is aimed at truth. For that reason, we do not have voluntary control over intellect in cases where our cognitive capacities, acting according to their nature, have been abundantly convinced of the truth of something.[16]

WISDOM AS ONE OF THE INTELLECTUAL VIRTUES

With this background on Aquinas's views of the will and the will's relations to intellect, we can now turn to his account of wisdom. Aquinas divides intellect or reason into theoretical reason and practical reason, and he assigns three virtues to the former and two to the latter.[17] The two virtues of practical intellect are prudence and art. Prudence has to do with reasoning about things that are to be done in order to obtain human good; art has to do with reasoning about things to be made in order to obtain human good.[18] The three virtues of the speculative intellect are wisdom, scientia, and understanding.[19] Understanding is a matter of grasping first principles, the starting points for the various sorts of sciences. Scientia involves comprehension of the causes of things and recognition of the ways things are related to their causes. Wisdom consists in understanding the highest (or as we would say, most fundamental) causes of everything and seeing everything else in the world in its relation to

---

[14] I take the notion of a design plan of cognitive faculties from Alvin Plantinga's fruitful and complex account; see his *Warrant and Proper Function*. (Oxford: Oxford University Press, 1993).

[15] Of course, on Aquinas's account of the relations between intellect and will, an act of will is dependent on some act of intellect (whether tacit or explicit) apprehending something as good. What is not clear is whether Aquinas thinks that the intellect's apprehension is the only constraint on the will in its relations to the other powers it can command, or whether he recognizes as well what seems clearly to be the case, namely, that acts of will are also constrained by the nature of the power or faculty or body part being commanded. Since the latter point is not only true but also common sensical and reasonably obvious, I will assume that it is part of what Aquinas has in mind here.

[16] *ST* I-II q.17 a.6.

[17] See, for example, *ST* I-II q.57 a.2 and a.4.

[18] *ST* I-II q.57 a.2.

[19] Scientia is often translated as 'knowledge', but in my view this is a misleading translation; see my "Aquinas on the Foundations of Knowledge", *Canadian Journal of Philosophy*, supplementary volume 17 (1991) 125-158. (For a somewhat different approach to Aquinas's account of scientia, see Scott MacDonald, "Theory of Knowledge", in *The Cambridge Companion to Aquinas*, ed. Norman Kretzmann and Eleonore Stump, (Cambridge: Cambridge University Press, 1993) 160-195.) In order to avoid adjudicating complex issues with a translation, I will leave the word untranslated. In my view, the least misleading way to translate 'scientia' is as 'science', where it is understood that science can encompass, e.g., metaphysics.

those highest (most fundamental) causes.[20]

What one thinks these highest causes are, and consequently what one thinks wisdom is, depends on the rest of one's world view. Aquinas, who knew Aristotle did not hold a world view identical with his own, supposes that for Aristotle the grasp of the most fundamental causes belongs to metaphysics (where metaphysics includes some natural theology), so that, Aquinas thinks, for Aristotle wisdom is a matter of mastering metaphysics.[21] For Aquinas himself, the highest or most fundamental cause is, of course, God, so that on Aquinas's account wisdom is a matter of knowing God's nature, God's actions, and God's decrees.[22] Just as we today suppose that any science will be understood best if the scientist begins with a solid foundation in physics and sees the other sciences in the light of that foundation, so Aquinas supposes that physics and all the sciences, including metaphysics, will be understood most deeply and most excellently by someone who has a good grasp of God's nature and actions. We and Aquinas, then, share the conviction that there is a hierarchy of knowledge about the world and that a cognitive agent's knowledge is held with more depth and richness if she knows the foundations (or as Aquinas would say, the pinnacle) of that hierarchy. On his view, the foundation, or the pinnacle, consists in the attributes and actions of the creator of the world, and knowing these is an intellectual virtue.

WISDOM AND CHARITY

There is more to the story of wisdom than this, however. Because of the nature of the highest cause on Aquinas's view --namely, God whose nature is identical with goodness -- Aquinas thinks that wisdom can make decisive judgments not only about God but also about the nature of the good and about the way in which other things are related to the good. In particular, wisdom can judge human acts in their relation to goodness. That is, wisdom can discern good or right actions from bad or wrong actions. For this reason, strictly speaking, wisdom is an excellence not just of the speculative intellect but of the practical

---

[20] See, for example, *ST* I-II q.66 a.5; also, *Sententia super Posteriora analytica* (In PA) II.20.15, *Sententia libri Ethicorum* (In NE) VI.6.1190 and 1193, and *Quaestiones disputatae de potentia* (QDP) 1.4

[21] As Aquinas of course understood, some of what is included in Aristotelian metaphysics is what we now would think of as philosophical theology. See, for example, *ST* II-II q.19 a.7.

[22] The discussion of Aristotle here and in the next sections should not obscure the fact that Aquinas's views of intellectual excellence in general and wisdom in particular have an Augustinian root as well. For some discussion of the way in which Aquinas and Augustine are related here, see, for example, Mark Jordan, *Ordering Wisdom: The Hierarchy of Philosophical Discourses in Aquinas.* (Notre Dame: University of Notre Dame Press, 1986), 122ff.

intellect as well.[23]

This view of Aquinas's helps explain the way in which he relates wisdom to the theological virtues, faith, hope, and charity. According to Aquinas, charity gives rise to wisdom and is accompanied by it. Now charity for Aquinas is love of God; but since on Aquinas's account God is identical with goodness, charity on his view is also a love of goodness,[24] and, for my purposes here, I will understand it in this way. On Aquinas's view, charity or a love of goodness is a prerequisite for wisdom. Taken in this way, wisdom is incompatible with any mortal sin, Aquinas says.[25] A person who is guilty of pride, envy, wrath, sloth, avarice, gluttony, or lust -- or of the lesser mortal sins which flow from these -- will undermine or destroy wisdom in herself. So according to Aquinas here, an excellence of the intellect is dependent on the will's being in a certain moral state.

The vice opposed to wisdom is, of course, folly; and folly, on Aquinas's view, has its source in what he calls lust. Although the Latin translated 'lust' ('luxuria') can be taken as narrowly as the contemporary English term 'lust', often something broader than lack of restraint with respect to sexual desire is intended. In the broader sense, the term refers to lack of self-discipline with regard to any desires for earthly things when those desires are morally unacceptable. Kicking your dog at the end of an exasperating day is thus an example of lust since the desire to take out your frustrations by kicking the dog is a desire which it is never acceptable to act on. Folly, like wisdom, is a condition of the intellect. But the fact that Aquinas thinks folly arises from lust shows us that folly, like wisdom, is also tied to states of the will.

Perhaps the first thing to strike our notice here is how far we are from wisdom in the Aristotelian sense of the mastery of metaphysics. The mastery of metaphysics, we naturally suppose, could be had by anyone in any moral or emotional state. It could be had by Hitler, for example, and on a day when he was characterized more by malice than by a passion for goodness. But Aquinas links together an excellence of the intellect with moral goodness in the will; and he supposes that the opposite of that intellectual excellence, namely, folly, is a concomitant of moral defects in the will.

On Aquinas's account of wisdom, then, a person's moral wrongdoing will

---

[23] *ST* II-II q.45 a.3.

[24] See, for example, *De veritate* q.14 a.8 ad 10. I am grateful to Norman Kretzmann for calling this passage to my attention.

[25] In *ST* II-II q.45 a.4 reply, Aquinas says that although wisdom which is an intellectual virtue can be in a person guilty of mortal sin, wisdom which is a gift cannot. Wisdom in this sense presupposes charity, and charity cannot occur together with mortal sin. (It is because charity can occur together with venial sin that venial sin does not preclude wisdom.) In that same question a.6 ad 3, Aquinas says because wisdom not only contemplates divine things but also regulates human acts, it requires distancing oneself from evil, which is incompatible with wisdom. That is why fear of God is the beginning of wisdom, because fear initiates the distancing from evils.

produce deficiencies in both her speculative and her practical intellect. That is, it will make her less capable of doing theology and ethics, and it will also undermine her practical intellect, leaving her prone not only to wrong moral judgments but also to self-deception. She will think her standards are appropriate and her judgments are correct when they are not. In other words, morally wrong choices on the part of the will produce defects in the intellect, so that the agent's moral judgments, moral theory, and theology contain mistakes, resulting in errors in conscience and concomitant self-deception on the agent's part. Furthermore, if we remember Aquinas's account of the dynamic interaction between intellect and will, we can see that this is not the end of the story. On Aquinas's understanding of the relations between intellect and will, the defective intellect will itself result in further wrong choices on the part of the will, which in turn will lead to further defects in the intellect, and so on in a vicious cycle. If this process gets bad enough, it results in the vice opposed to wisdom, namely, folly. And I think we will understand Aquinas's idea here best if we focus on what he has to say about folly.[26]

WISDOM AND FOLLY

By way of a general characterization of folly, Aquinas says that it implies a certain apathy of heart and dullness of mind.[27] What is more interesting, I think, are the various descriptions he gives of the fool. He presents three of them, all taken from Isidore of Seville: a fool is one who through dullness remains unmoved; a fool is one who is unconcerned when he is injured; and a fool is one whom shame does not incite to sorrow.[28] What do these claims about the fool mean, and what do they have to do with the way in which wisdom is supposed to be undermined by moral wrongdoing?

I think it is most helpful here to begin with a particular case taken from popular storytelling. So think about the recent movie *What's Love Got to Do With It?* and the story of Ike and Tina Turner. (I am not really interested in Ike and Tina's history here, so I am just going to assume that the movie is telling

---

[26] Because I explicate wisdom by focusing on folly and because in folly will exercises only immediate indirect control over intellect, someone might suppose that Aquinas needs only the weaker claim, that will has such indirect control, and not also the stronger claim, that will has direct control over intellect. But this is a misimpression generated by my explication of wisdom in terms of its opposed vice, folly. The process by which will corrupts intellect does require only indirect control over intellect on the part of the will. But the process by which will and intellect function together to produce wisdom has as an essential ingredient direct control by the will over the intellect. Wisdom is an outgrowth of charity, which in turn depends on faith; and faith is a case in which will exercises direct control over intellect, on Aquinas's view. If there were space here to explicate Aquinas's entire account of wisdom, it would, consequently, be clear that the stronger claim is necessary.

[27] *ST* II-II q.45 a.6.

[28] Ibid.

the truth in every detail. If that assumption is false, then what is said here should be taken as a fictional example, rather than a historical one.) According to the movie, Tina -- or Anna Mae (her real name) -- is a terrific person and a talented musician, a loving mother and a devoted wife, a beautiful woman and a highly popular performer. Ike, on the other hand, has a limited talent and is a rotten person besides. He is a drinker and a drug addict; he is not only unfaithful to Anna Mae but he is a womanizer; and worst of all, he is a brute of a husband, who from time to time beats Anna Mae unmercifully.

After the movie was released, various media people contacted Ike, who had just been released from prison where he was serving time for a conviction on drug charges. Was the movie portrayal of him accurate, the reporters wanted to know? Did he really beat Anna Mae in that way? Yes, he said, he did, but it was no big deal; he only slapped her around when she made him really mad. Was he really such a womanizer? Well, he said, he did sleep around a lot when he was married to Anna Mae, but none of those other women really meant anything to him. And so the interviews went. Ike Turner is a man who lost his one shot at glory, who through no fault but his own lost a talented, beautiful, internationally acclaimed woman who was devoted to him, and whose utterly shameful actions have been portrayed in revolting detail for movie audiences throughout the country. And what is his reaction to what has happened to him and the way in which he has been portrayed? His reaction from start to finish seems to be this: "Sure, I did the things the movie portrays me as doing, but it's not a big deal!" In fact, his agent says that Ike is contemplating a movie telling his side of the story. In his movie, no doubt, he will beat his wife bloody, but audiences will get to see that she was making him mad when he did it.

What should we think about Ike Turner? Our first reaction is likely to be moral revulsion. His behavior towards Anna Mae is outrageous; he is verbally, emotionally, and physically abusive towards her. But what is more interesting from our point of view here is Ike's reaction to the release of the movie, which he acknowledges to be basically accurate as regards his actions, if not his motivation. His reputation in the country fell precipitously; the movie did him incalculable damage in a host of respects ranging from financial and professional to personal and emotional. Now shame is a matter of a person's recognition that others hold a morally low opinion of him, when that low opinion is correct. A shamed person, in other words, is someone who ought to have low self-esteem and who recognizes that other people see him in this way. (This is a sense of 'shame' in which a person can be shamed without feeling ashamed.)[29] So we might say of Ike Turner that the release of the movie has

---

[29] Perhaps the paradigm cases of shame are those in which a person shares with a selected set of the public around him a correct morally low opinion of himself. But while it seems necessary for shame that the low opinion be correct, it isn't necessary that the shamed person should understand the low opinion to be correct. Ike Turner is shamed, even if he can't

both shamed and injured him. But what is frustrating and obnoxious about his response to the movie is that he does not seem to care. His response is "No big deal." In other words, Ike fits Aquinas's (and Isidore's) definition of a fool. Shame is not inciting him to any sorrow over what he has done or what he has become, and he is not taking deeply to heart the injury the movie is doing him.

Ike Turner's condition here is not unrepresentative of what we find, I think, when we look at people habituated to major moral evil and then brought face to face with moral condemnation in others. Think about white South Africans supporting apartheid, or think about Eichmann at his trial in Jerusalem or think about the Bosnian Serbs. Like Ike Turner, they seem to fit Aquinas's definition of a fool: the shame their actions elicit evokes no sorrow for those actions in them, and the injury done them by their shaming does not evoke in them any deep moral concern. The camp doctor at Auschwitz, Johann Paul Kremer, personally murdered many people in dreadful scientific experiments. In his diaries, published after the war, he details both his murders and his opinion of himself as an upstanding citizen, a devoted family man, a morally good person. He thinks of himself as a person of great moral sensitivity even as he notes the pain and suffering he causes the Jews in the camp.[30] Nothing about his public disgrace at his two trials and convictions after the war seems to have changed his mind.[31] In Aquinas's sense, he is a paradigm of a fool. The elders in the story of Susanna are like this also. As the elders themselves can see, the evil of each one is clearly revealed to others, first to the other elder and then to Susanna.[32] Furthermore, since nothing in the story suggests that they are atheists, each elder presumably also supposes that God sees his evil

---

recognize that the low opinion people have of him is right. Some people might suppose that the requirement that the low opinion be correct is similarly unnecessary. But this view doesn't seem right. Socrates wasn't shamed at his trial, although lots of people there apparently held a morally low opinion of him, just because their low opinion was incorrect. In cases where a person shares with others a low opinion of himself which he and they erroneously suppose to be correct, it seems to me better to describe such a person as humiliated, rather than as shamed. It is a consequence of this way of thinking about shame that a person can be mistaken in thinking that he is shamed. Finally, if we suppose that there are cases in which a person has a correct low opinion of himself and there is no one else (not even God) who shares it with him, it seems to me better to speak of low self-esteem or maybe humility, rather than shame.

[30] His diary is available in English translation in Jadwiga Bezwinska and Danuta Czech, *KL Auschwitz Seen by the SS*. Hoess, Broad, Kremer, (New York: Howard Fertig, 1984).

[31] Johann Paul Kremer, previously an anatomy professor at the University of Muenster, came to Auschwitz in August 1942. After the war, he was tried in Poland and sentenced to death, but because of his age the sentence was commuted to ten years. On his release, he returned to Muenster, where he created a stir by trying to portray himself as a martyr to the German cause. The upshot was that he was tried in Muenster and convicted a second time. See Bezwinska and Czech, *KL Auschwitz...*, op.cit., 8.

[32] *AB*, 93-94: "after quizzing one another ..., they admitted their passion."

too. But neither elder is moved to any remorse or sorrow by the knowledge that his evil is known to others who see it as the evil it is. Neither elder shows any internal anguish or moral pain. Each simply persists without contrition to finish the evil course he has begun, attempting to bring about Susanna's death because she will not give in to his adulterous desires. The elders, then, also fit Aquinas's definition of a fool. The shame of having their evil known generates no moral sorrow in them.

THE PROGRESSION OF EVIL

Here, then, we return to the question with which this paper began: How does a person get to be in such a morally frightening condition? Nazis are made; they are not born. The most insightful study of the making of a Nazi is Gita Sereny's biography of Franz Stangl, the commandant of Treblinka.[33] She shows the way in which each serious instance of moral wrongdoing on Stangl's part made it easier for him to take the next and further step into moral evil; the move into moral monstrosity is slow and gradual.

When he was first assigned to head a euthanasia clinic, Stangl was morally repelled by what the Nazis were doing. But he was afraid that he would lose his job or even his position among the Nazis if he made any trouble, and so he talked himself into thinking first that the euthanasia was a necessary evil and then that it was in fact a favor to those killed.[34] Having dulled himself in this way, he found it easier to take the next step into evil, where again he had to choose between, on the one hand, losing his promotion or his position or even his security in the system and, on the other, losing further moral ground. In each case, he protected his position and security at the cost of morality. Nothing in his trial or his consequent disgrace and prison term could shake his conviction that in all his actions he was a morally good person, even a humane and morally sensitive person, who did what he did just because he was following orders, in a morally appropriate spirit of civic and military obedience. Nothing about the revulsion in which he was held by the whole world gave him any serious pause.

Aquinas's account of wisdom and folly give the theoretical background for the example in Gita Sereny's study, and his theory of the relation between intellect and will provides the underlying explanation of how a person can become a moral monster such as Stangl was.[35]

---

[33] Gita Sereny, *Into That Darkness. An Examination of Conscience.* (New York: First Vintage Books Edition, 1983). Also helpful in this connection is Robert Jay Lifton, *The Nazi Doctors*. (New York: Basic Books, 1986), especially the pages on socialization, pp. 193-213.

[34] Sereny 1983, 48ff.

[35] I am not trying to argue that the only way in which to interpret Stangl's case is in terms of Aquinas's theory of wisdom and folly. My point is only that Stangl's story is a good illustration for Aquinas's theory and that Aquinas's theory provides a helpful elucidation of Stangl's story.

Like the elders in the story of Susanna, though clearly in a radically more serious way, Stangl is a fool, a person whom shame does not incite to sorrow and who is unconcerned when he is injured. He has a severely impaired speculative intellect, unable to apprehend the highest causes of things, including the nature of goodness; and in consequence his practical intellect is also grossly deficient in its ability to make particular moral judgments. The result is that he is self-deceived and morally monstrous. What has brought him to this condition is a disinclination, made habitual from long practice, to discipline his desires for worldly well-being when they conflict with morality -- or luxuria, in the broad medieval sense described above.

And the reason these morally wrong choices can have the effect of misprogramming the intellect in both its speculative and its practical parts is explained by the dynamic interaction of will and intellect and by will's ability to exercise control over intellect.

Stangl wants to accept his appointment at the euthanasia institute, or, at any rate, he prefers doing so to the other alternatives open to him; but he is also horrified by the nature of the assignment. In the beginning, he is double-minded, wavering between thinking he must accept the assignment and thinking that he will not be able to stick it out. "After the first two or three days," Stangl told Sereny, "...I didn't think I could stand it. ....I ...couldn't eat -- you know, one just couldn't".[36] In the end, however, he does -- all things considered -- want to accept and remain in his assignment. As Aquinas holds, though, a wrong action can be willed by the will only in case the intellect has succeeded in finding some description under which it seems good.[37] And so in a case in which the will wants what in fact is not good, it directs the attention of the intellect to just the evidence which supports the goodness of what it wants, and it turns the intellect away from any countervailing evidence.

This seems a fairly good description of what happened in Stangl's case. Sereny asks him whether he succeeded in convincing himself that what he was doing was right. Yes, he explains, he did so in virtue of reflecting on an encounter he had with a Catholic nun, who was in favor of euthanasia for disabled children. Speaking of a severely disabled sixteen-year old child who was not taken for euthanasia, the nun said, "Just look at him... No good to himself or anyone else. How could they refuse to deliver him from this

---

[36] Sereny 1983, 55.

[37] See, for example, *ST* I-II q.19 a.3, where Aquinas explains that the will's object is always proposed to it by reason, so that understood good (as distinct from what is really good) is what the will wants. See also *ST* I-II q.15 a.3 where Aquinas explains the progression towards action in this way: intellect's apprehension of the end, the desire of the end, counsel about the means, and the desire of the means. Also *ST* I-II q.74 a.7 ad 1, ad 2, and ad 3, where Aquinas says that consent to sin is an act of the appetitive power in consequence of an act of reason, so that reason's approving as good something which is in fact not good precedes sinful acts. Finally, in *ST* I-II q.75 a.2 he explains that the cause of sin is some apparent good, and therefore both intellect and will play a role in sinning.

miserable life?" Commenting on this speech by the nun, tacitly approved by an accompanying priest, Stangl says, "Here was a Catholic nun, a Mother Superior, and a priest. And they thought it was right. Who was I then, to doubt what was being done?".[38] Here will has directed intellect to reflect on this one encounter and on the fact that the person who gave moral approval to euthanasia was a person whose office generally carries moral authority, namely, a nun. On the other hand, there was abundant evidence available to Stangl to indicate that many Protestant and Catholic clergy were strongly opposed to euthanasia.[39] He finds euthanasia morally acceptable on the basis of one nun's approval of it only because his will is also directing the attention of his intellect away from the countervailing evidence.[40]

Because he has succeeded in approving euthanasia as morally acceptable or even morally good, he has to this extent misprogrammed his intellect, and the next step is easier to take. The misprogrammed intellect allows will to want as good what it might have rejected before the misprogramming of the intellect; and the warped will, in turn, misprograms the intellect further. So will and intellect are in a dynamic interaction which allows each of them to corrupt the other, one step at a time. Aquinas's theory, then, makes it easier to understand the well-documented fact that the descent into moral monstrousness tends to be gradual rather than precipitous, and it also shows, at least in part, how it is that conscience becomes dulled.

This is what we find in the case of the elders also. They begin by lusting in their hearts.[41] From that point they progress to sharing their lustful thoughts with each other --sinning in word and not just in thought. Then they determine to exercise their lust in act, going one step further still. Their determination to satisfy their lust by coercing Susanna, rather than by trying to seduce her or

---

[38] Sereny 1983, 58.

[39] Sereny documents the part religious authorities played in both condoning and condemning the Nazi euthanasia program, and the degree to which Germans, Stangl included, were aware of church attitudes towards euthanasia. For example, she quotes Frau Stangl's claim that she discussed with her husband a widely publicized sermon by the Bishop of Munster condemning euthanasia. (59).

[40] It helps, of course, in this process that the Nazis were so careful with language. The higher-up who assigned Stangl to the euthanasia institute spoke to him in abstract and high-flown language, and Stangl records his distress at having to deal with a superior who did not observe such linguistic conventions: "My heart sank when I met him. ...[he had] this awful verbal crudity; when he spoke about the necessity for this euthanasia operation, he was not speaking in humane or scientific terms, the way Dr. Werner had described it to me. ... He spoke of 'doing away with useless mouths' and said that 'sentimental slobber' about such people made him 'puke'." (54). Clearly, the Nazi gift for Orwellian misdescription made it easier to misprogram the intellect in the way Aquinas thinks necessary for moral evil. In this connection, see also Robert Jay Lifton, *The Nazi Doctors.*, op.cit., 202-203 and 445-446.

[41] *AB*, 93: "Both were lovesick for her; but they did not tell one another of their frustration since they were ashamed to admit their passion, that they wanted to have intercourse with her."

bribe her, for example, takes them still another step further into evil. And so it goes, till we find them at the end perverting morality, law, and religion in their attempt to bring about Susanna's death.[42]   The same progression is evident in the case of many of the Nazis. Stangl went from the euthanasia institute at Hartheim to one at Bernburg, where those "eligible" for euthanasia included perfectly healthy political prisoners. And from there he went to Lublin where he was gradually inducted into the secrets of the death camps until he accepted the assignment of supervising Sobibor. When Sereny asked him how he felt when he first came in contact with the gassing of Jews at Sobibor, he answered, "At Sobibor one could avoid seeing almost all of it".[43]   In Treblinka, he could not help but see it, and he called what he saw "Dante['s Inferno] come to life"; but he accepted his posting as commandant to that death camp.[44]   In response to Sereny's question how he could have stilled his conscience into accepting, he said, "the only way I could live was by compartmentalizing my thinking"[45] -- by which he meant willing not to think about a great deal.

With every wrong action, then, there is a misprogramming of the intellect; and the misprogrammed intellect twists the will, which in turn misprograms the intellect further.   These misprogrammings can be both progressive and cumulative, till they reach the point where a man like Stangl, who at first almost could not bear the painless death of the severely disabled, subsequently was able to oversee with a quietened conscience tortures and killings that now sicken those who just read pale descriptions of them.[46]

Furthermore, breaking into the cycle of the spiraling corruption of intellect and will, on Aquinas's account, clearly will be difficult. The outrage of virtually the whole civilized world was not enough to turn Stangl from his conviction that he had never been responsible for any serious evil, that he had always done what he ought to have done in the circumstances. The shame of his internationally publicized trial and the deluge of shaming publications documenting his part in mass murder inspired him to no repentance or moral sorrow.

Why this should be so is easier to see on Aquinas's theory of intellect and will. A severely misprogrammed intellect with correspondingly twisted will and desires will be hard to fix, because the misprogramming will have to be undone, one piece at a time, but this will be an undoing for which the agent has no will

---

[42] *AB*, 101: "the two elders arrived, viciously determined to have [Susanna] put to death. ... Inasmuch as they were elders of the people and judges, the entire congregation believed them and condemned Susanna to death."

[43] Sereny 1983, 114.

[44] Sereny 1983, 157.

[45] Sereny 1983, 164.

[46] I do not mean to imply that this interaction between intellect and will is all there is to say about the descent into evil. For some excellent discussion of associated factors, see Robert Jay Lifton, *The Nazi Doctors.*, op.cit., 418-465.

or desire, or which his will is even set against. Consequently, the corrupting interaction of will and intellect will continue. In his self-deceived state, Stangl does not see his actions or himself as the rest of the world does, and he does not want to do so either. That is why shame produces no sorrow in him. One of the worst things about our moral evil, from Aquinas's point of view, is that it makes us into fools.

So from Aquinas's point of view, the elders in the story of Susanna are not cardboard caricatures of bad people. Rather they show us the human state of moral monstrousness that Aquinas thinks is part of folly. Furthermore, the story portrays realistically how the elders come to be in that despicable and desperate condition. By failing to discipline their original desires when what they were desiring was not morally acceptable, they engaged in a process of corruption, with will misprogramming intellect and intellect warping will, which in turn misprogrammed intellect further, in an on-going progression of moral evil, till they ended as fools.

WISDOM: DANIEL AND SUSANNA

With this understanding of the nature of wisdom and folly, let us look again at the traditional characterization of Daniel and Susanna in the story. Susanna has regularly been taken to exemplify chastity and patience in suffering, as I said at the beginning of this paper, and Daniel is understood as the paradigm of wisdom. But if we bring Aquinas's sophisticated understanding of wisdom to bear on the story, it does not seem properly found in Daniel in those actions for which he is praised in the story.

Wisdom, as Aquinas has been arguing, involves an understanding of the good and an ability to discern correctly which human actions are good, with a consequent willing of those good actions. We might suppose that Daniel's own moral goodness is responsible for the fact that he cares about a fair trial. This view of Daniel is no doubt correct. But what motivates Daniel's particular actions in the story is a sense on his part that the trial has gone much too quickly, that the people have failed to cross-examine the witnesses and are acting hastily.[47] The cross-examination of the witnesses which he then conducts is cleverly designed to detect whether their stories coincide or not. Daniel shows considerable acumen in refusing to accept the surface appearances at the trial, and he is clever is determining a way to get at the truth. We today might put the point by saying that Daniel is very smart. But smart is not the same as wise, and acumen and cleverness are insufficient for wisdom. Even a corrupt but clever lawyer might do what Daniel did; special moral discernment is not needed here.

Special moral discernment is needed and is shown in Susanna's case,

---

[47] *AB*, 106: Daniel says, "Are you such fools, sons of Israel? Would you condemn a daughter of Israel without first cross-examining and discovering its accuracy?".

however. From the fact that two men of weighty religious authority try to coerce her into a certain action, she might conclude that action is not nearly as morally wrong as she herself was initially inclined to suppose. She might have reasoned, that is, as Stangl did at the euthanasia institute, when he came to regard euthanasia as morally acceptable in consequence of the fact that a priest and a nun were in favor of it. Or she might have concluded that giving in to the elders would be wrong but that she lived in a society where such wrongs were so much part of the social fabric that she could not do anything about them; she had just to accept them. This, too, was a very common moral reaction during the Nazi period, even on the part of some otherwise decent people. Or finally she might have decided that if she had to choose between saving her life or resisting some great moral evil, saving her life was always the greater good.

As the story tells it, however, Susanna makes none of these morally weak and self-serving judgments. Pressured by the elders, surprised and frightened, with no time for cool reason to survey and contemplate all the options, she turns on the instant to the morally heroic choice: she will put her life on the line to avoid collaborating with moral evil. In this choice she exemplifies the special excellence of intellect and will that Aquinas calls wisdom. She sees with clarity what is good and right to do, even under severe pressure to rationalize otherwise, and seeing it, she wants it, even at the cost of risking her life. In an instant, then, she grasps the moral point it took Stangl his whole life to understand: "I should have died," Stangl said at the end of his life, "that is my guilt." And while he might be exaggerating the cost to himself of resistance, he is surely right in the general point. Death would have been better than the moral evil he engaged in. Susanna had only a moment to make her decision, and she made it in the right way, with wisdom. "I would rather fall into your hands," she tells the elders, "than sin against the Lord."[48] And so Susanna, in her suffering and her patience, not Daniel in his lawyerly power and triumph, exemplifies wisdom for us.[49]

---

[48] *AB*, 94.

[49] Some parts of this paper are taken from a much longer paper on Aquinas, "Wisdom: Will, Belief, and Moral Goodness", forthcoming in *Aquinas's Moral Theory.*, ed. Scott MacDonald and Eleonore Stump, Cornell University Press. I am grateful for the stimulating discussion this paper received at the conference on *Susanna and the Elders*, and I am indebted to Ellen Spolsky for her excellent work in putting the conference together; I am also grateful to Norman Kretzmann for many helpful comments and suggestions on an earlier draft of this paper.

Law or the Garden:
The Betrayal of Susanna in Pastoral Painting

Ellen Spolsky
Bar-Ilan University

The story I want to tell is about how Daniel rescued Susanna from the Elders, and how Rembrandt lost her again. It is an old story of the conflict between beauty and truth. Looked at as Jewish cultural history, it is a story of the conflict between the Pharisees and the Hellenizers. Looked at as Western cultural history it is a story of the romance between European painting and the Greek pastoral tradition. As pastoral, the paintings of Susanna bathing draw their appeal and their meaning from the realms of sensual pleasure, producing an unresolvable tension between different kinds of knowledge. The insertion of the story of *Susanna and the Elders* into the genre of pastoral is, thus, an entanglement with skepticism.[1] I will argue here, as I examine the visual dynamics among painters, viewers, and the three figures in the garden, that whatever gain the paintings of Susanna and the Elders represent for art history is offset by a loss for truth, for law, and for the image of women as independent human beings whose virtue is not prima facie in doubt. The switch from verbal to visual media, for this story at least, entails the abandonment of the struggle to live ethically in a complicated world.

In the earliest version of the story now extant, in Old Greek, and presumed to originate in the Jewish community in Alexandria, the young prophet Daniel is inspired to a legal intervention by means of which he rescues Susanna from slander and the distortion of justice. Her husband's private garden, which should have been a sheltered retreat, had become a prison to her; she had been locked in there by the combination of her own natural beauty and the lust and irresponsibility of men with civic power on their side. In the later

---

[1] The connection between skepticism and the pastoral in early modern literature and painting is the subject of a book I am now completing called *Satisfaction*.

101

Greek version of the story, perhaps by Theodotion[2], we can already see the influence of the Greek erotic romance. The European paintings are based on this revision, not on the earlier version, and the result is clearly regressive. Having been entered into the ambiance of the Greek pastoral, the story of Daniel's accomplishment is vitiated: his triumph had been in using his intelligence to defend truth and virtue, but the pastoral is necessarily deeply skeptical of the power of intelligence. Its interests are primarily sensual, in the pursuit of which it severs the connection between rationality and ethical behavior.

The paintings are the evidence of the change. The *raison d'etre* of all the paintings, of course, is the representation of Susanna's beauty. By their choice of subject matter alone, then, the painters are caught committing the Elders' own sin. They picture her naked beauty on canvas as the Elders pictured it in their minds' eyes.[3] Several of the paintings add further dimensions of pleasure - pleasure, that is, for the male viewer - which is more readily available from paintings than from text. In the paintings by Tintoretto (Fig. 1) and Guercino (Fig. 2), and in several versions of the scene painted by Veronese, for example, the presence of conventional references to Venus (mirrors, jewels, peacocks, cupids), suggests that the beauty of the woman be read as mitigation of the Elders' crime. In these pictures Susanna is unaware of the concealed elders, although the viewer sees their ugly faces and prominent hands. Their posture and their facial expressions are distorted, but she is self-possessed, relaxed in her ablutions, with limbs gracefully extended: all *"lux, calme, et volupte"*. Her obliviousness to their presence emphasizes her charmingly childish self-absorption. In the Guercino, the Elder is grasping a stick, visually analogous to his male member. As we can see from his upright position, he is indeed holding or restraining himself from moving toward Susanna. He seems to be immobilized by her loveliness, painted as a halo of light around her. The Elder standing above him faces out of the picture and raises a pointed finger - conventionally in these pictures to silence Susanna (see Fig. 4) but here extended toward the viewer, as if to say "Don't disturb her" -and at the same time, "Don't be so quick to judge us - wouldn't you also be enchanted by her?"

Thus, at the same time as the painting itself is an *objet d'art*, the painted

---

[2] *The Anchor Bible*'s volume containing both texts of Susanna, edited by Carey A. Moore, provides the fullest textual notes and most up to date scholarly apparatus on the texts. See Moore, p.31 for the difficulties of this widely assumed attribution.

[3] The painters, in some of the paintings, seem to exculpate the viewer, if not the elders, from the blame that might be incurred by enjoying the sight of the naked bather. Michael Fried cites Diderot's claim that the subject matter of Susanna reinforces the convention of painting by which, as in the theater, the pretense is made that there is no beholder. Here the subject itself is "illicit beholding." According to Diderot, by including the elders in the painting, and having her attempt to cover herself from their view, "Susannah is chaste and so is the painter. Neither one nor the other knew I was there." (1980:96)

Figure 1. Tintoretto, c. 1557 Kunsthistorisches Museum, Vienna

woman is also an object, available to the viewer's gaze. His stare might be illicit, but the painter helps him over his guilt, as it were, by picturing her nudity as vanity; her preening legitimates his gaze, and she is thus made accessible to the viewer. The genre of the paintings further enfranchises the viewer: he is forgiven, as it were, by the pastoral. Taken into its world view, he is relieved of the burden of making moral judgments. Thus in spite of the textual assertions of her innocence, Tintoretto's Susanna is both a figure of Vanitas and a part of the natural landscape, available for the holiday enjoyment of the viewer. One can understand those feminist art critics who see the painting as a highly sophisticated version of the old "she asked for it" line.[4]

Some of the pictures, e.g., the Hague Rembrandt (Fig. 3), capture a different moment: that at which she becomes aware of an intruder. She is now crouching to cover her nakedness (though ineffectually), her face turned in fear, looking over her shoulder to identify the threat. Here, a frisson is added to the

---

[4] See Gill Saunders, 1989. Martin Braun says "it is a commonplace of Hellenistic-Oriental literature that the woman adorns herself lavishly to seduce a youth...." See, e.g., *Talmud Bavli Yoma*, 35b on Potiphar's wife: "the Egyptian woman changed apparel twice daily to find favour with Joseph" (1938: 86-87).

Figure 2. Guercino, 1617 Museo del Prado, Madrid

eroticism of the pictured body, caused by the impression of its vulnerability. It is difficult not to see the painter's choice of this moment as sadistic; the viewer is allowed to enjoy her shock and fear.

Though viewing is, as Mieke Bal claims, a metonym for touching (150), some of the pictures represent the abusive handling explicitly. If in these pictures the literalness of the grasp makes it easier for a male viewer to enjoy the attempted rape vicariously, at the same time, it is also easier for viewers to judge the guilt of the Elders. The ugly hand of one of the men pulls her garment away from her in the Domenichino painting (Fig. 4), and in the van Dyck (Fig. 5) coarse fingers, distorted with age, paw her shoulder. Several aspects of van Dyck's painting conspire to encourage the viewer's moral and emotional judgment of Susanna as the victim of the Elders' evil. A developing storm eclipses the light at the horizon. They are in darkness, she in light. They are overbearing, threatening, as they make their indecent proposal, both of them tugging on her garment, making it clear to her that she has no choice. Her pearls and rings that were, until the intrusion, innocent trinkets are now pushed aside, the jug (conventionally representing virginity or chastity) is now

Figure 3. Rembrandt, 1634 Moritshuis, The Hague

overturned - distorted, as is her facial expression, by fear of the ugliness forced upon her. However, even when the viewer cannot escape seeing the mens' sin, he is still allowed to enjoy her pain.

The eroticism of the European paintings of *Susanna and the Elders* is often acknowledged in art-historical discussion by the remark that the painters might well have taken their subject to be little more than an excuse to paint a

Figure 4. Domenichino, 1603 Galleria Villa Doria-Pamphilj, Rome

beautiful woman in the nude.[5] But the pictures I have reprinted here make it
impossible to accept the judgment of innocent naughtiness suggested by that
cliché. The pleasure of eroticism isn't all that is at stake. Most of the painters
acknowledge the dilemma of entrapment and guilt, while finding ways to make
it easier for a viewer to enjoy the beautiful woman and condemn the men in the
picture instead of himself. Blaming Susanna's vanity may offer relief, as does
the expedient of painting the Elders as Jews, as Others with turbans,
stereotypical large and ugly noses, and grasping hands.

The Domenichino Susanna (Fig. 4) pretends to take a strong moral
position, providing a large number of compositional and kinesthetic clues to
encourage the viewer to condemn the Elders, yet it still provides the viewer
with the means to commit a version of their sin. In the center of the
composition, Susanna's resistance is made explicit by the broad line of her
garment which is the subject of a tugging contest. She extends her right arm
across her body to the left in order to pull back the garment the turbaned Elder
nearest her is pulling away from her. Her left arm crosses her body to the right
in an effort to keep the drape over her lower torso. Crucially, she looks neither

---

[5] This cliche is repeated, for example, by Christopher Brown (1982) in his discussion of
van Dyck's Susanna, and by the anonymous writer of the article on Susanna of the
Encyclopaedia Judaica.

Figure 5. Anthony van Dyck, c.1620 Bayerischen
Staatsgemäldesammlungen, Munich

at the men nor at the viewer, but turns her eyes, indeed her whole face toward
heaven, demonstrating her knowledge that only God can help her.

Figure 6.   Rembrandt, 1645   Staatliche Museen - Preussischer
Kulturbesitz Gemäldegalerie, Berlin

Crouched over her with a finger to his lips, the Elder who is pulling her
drape with his other hand is at once cautioning her silence and demonstrating
that her crying out will be useless: it is so easy for him to disrobe her that he
doesn't even need his two hands to do it.   Insult is added to injury, as in the
story, by his assuming the role of adviser as if he were indeed her Elder, her
teacher, even as the content of his message is the uselessness of her crying out,
since he will in any case bear false witness.   The ultimate futility of his
silencing her, however, is emphasized by her upwardly turned eyes, as in
traditional paintings of martyrdom.   Her silence in the garden could only
provide short term cover; the only audience that matters is God.

Domenichino is not a subtle moralist. If you haven't got the message yet,
look at the second Elder. While the first elder is concerned with obtaining both
Susanna's garment and her collusion, the second is more forcefully
undisciplined, already having a knee over the balustrade.   He thus visually
crosses the moral boundary which should keep him away from someone else's

wife. Hatless and wide-eyed, he is set to lower the leg over the barrier and jump into that space in both picture and story where he doesn't belong.

Why should looking, beauty, power, and guilt, be so entangled here? Wendy Steiner describes this tension as between "voyeurism and vision, narcissism and love." (55) Beauty, as enchantment, has power over the viewer; Susanna's beauty seduces the Elders, and the painting's beauty enchants its viewers. Richard Pervo, writing about Greek romance, notes the same irony there: the beauty of women in the romances is such that their appearances "usually have the characteristics of an epiphany. Men are drawn to them as if by magnets. Their attractiveness seems to place them in positions of power, but they chiefly use it to extricate themselves from the difficulties it has created." (1991:146) Between the poles of worship and intrusion, whose looking is tribute, whose abuse?[6]

Leo Steinberg may have been the first to discuss the tension, in Picasso's drawings, between sleeping subjects (almost but not always women) and unobserved watchers. In the motif he calls "sleep watching," the sleeper (nude of course), is in the power of the alert watcher, "because sleep itself is a fragile condition." (1972:101) This imbalance of power, as in the case of the Elders who spy on Susanna, motivates a narrative. Yet, Steinberg points out, there can also be - sometimes at the same time - a wistful reversal. The female sleeper is dreaming - at peace, separated from the observer's wakeful desire. He is excluded. "Her sleep, so far from offering a main chance or licentious occasion, awakens the [watcher] to his banishment. The sleeper's withdrawal is recognized as a desertion. Which leaves the nymph newly empowered; no longer defenseless game, she holds the power of the kept secret, the power of the safe and the lock." (1972:101-102) This is a wonderful description of the combination of ideal beauty and pathos that can be read in Tintoretto's *Susanna*, in which she is unaware of the Elders, even though she is not asleep. The men here are simply no match for her bright wholeness. Pictorially marginalized (one in the far back and one in the left lower corner) they are clearly excluded from whatever it is she knows. The fence, in this case, succeeds in keeping them from her (cf. Fig. 4). The men do not reach out their hands. The man in the bottom left, in fact, like one of the figures in the Guercino (Fig. 2) actually restrains himself, pulling in his own garment, as if in recognition of his impotence in the face of the ideals of youth, beauty, and pleasure she represents. If, at some level, Susanna is being blamed here for being seductive, it is this picture that is most successful of them all in excusing the men as well as the woman herself for taking pleasure in sensual beauty.

Bal's articulation of the situation of the voyeuristic Elders in her discussion of Rembrandt's two Susannas adds further depth to Steinberg's description of the ambiguity of the power relationships within the picture. Bal

---

[6] Steiner (1988:48) notes correctly, in a subordinate clause, that "in a religious context" the power of illicit viewing may be considered idolatry.

argues that the content of the Elders' accusation of Susanna is a displaced wish-fulfillment: they accuse her, she notes, of their own desires. That is, of course, the nature of slander: since it didn't happen, it must be invented, envisioned, by the slanderer. Each of the old men has imagined himself a young man making love in the garden to the beautiful Susanna.

> The key phrase is "we saw them in the act." Seeing is hardly the pretended innocent witnessing in this context. They saw her while they were hiding, and, as viewers of pornography, desired/ fantasized the act. They hallucinated the act, performed by procuration in their stead, by someone young, stronger than them. (1991:153)

Bal thus sees Susanna as victim, noting also the judicial power of the Elders who are capable, their lust spurned, of having her sentenced to death. Steinberg's reading of Picasso, however, lets us see that she is not without her own power over them. They understand themselves aggrieved; they are indeed shut out of her world of beauty and pleasure. Their exclusion hints at the justice of her ultimate triumph. The Elders are surely victimizers, but also vulnerable, both because they are helpless to bring about their own satisfaction, except in their imaginations, and because by slandering they are vulnerable to the power of a law higher than the civil law they control and pervert. Visually, they are vulnerable simply because they are old. Who cannot smile at Domenichino's Elder with his knee over the balustrade, or Rembrandt's old man (Fig. 6) who seems to be holding back at the gate (clutching a stick) until he sees whether his more aggressive colleague has any success in pursuing the young girl? The behavior of the first is clownish, as if he has forgotten that he is not as young as he used to be. The second - is that a shadow of doubt on his face? - may, on the other hand, be remembering his age.

Susanna, however, who cannot counter their slander by speaking in her own defense at her trial, has even greater power over them, as Domenichino illustrates, by speaking directly to God:

> Then Susanna cried out with a loud voice, and said, O everlasting God, that knowest the secrets, and knowest all things before they be: thou knowest that they have borne false witness against me...

"And the Lord heard her voice," immediately appointing as his agent none less than a prophet, the young Daniel, who becomes her spokesperson. Indeed a young man seizes her: he takes her out of their corrupt jurisdiction, to be judged, as it were, in a higher court. That the Elders suffer, measure for measure, the punishment of death, having as comfort only their dreams of illicit behavior, shows that the balance of power is, in the story, if not always or clearly in the paintings, in the woman's favor.

The artist paints only one scene, and Daniel is almost never present.[7] The pictorial tradition overwhelmingly prefers the portrayal of the woman at her bath, in a lovely garden setting, over the representation of a trial scene. The painter, seduced by the beauty of the imagined body of the woman, himself repeats the lust of the Elders, and in turn lures the viewer into that same sin. Even the critic, and even when she is a woman, seems bound to repeat the exploitation by reprinting the pictures. There is, however, still plenty to learn from the texts at hand.

When we look at the Theodotion translation, the later and fuller of the two, we see that it is not entirely fair to place all the blame for the distortion of the story's teaching on the painters. Their interpretations of the story were derived from the apocryphal story to which they had access - itself a focally Greek romance. The story in the Apocrypha of the Christian Bible was based on this text. The context of the translation of the Hebrew Scriptures into Greek is relevant here. It was begun under the patronage of Ptolemy II, Philadelphus, in the middle of the third century B.C.E. This same king is credited with establishing the library at Alexandria, and patronized one of the earliest Greek writers of pastoral verse, Theocritus. By the time of Theodotion's retranslation of the story of Susanna into Greek, probably at the end of the 2nd century, C.E., the genre of popular, erotic, pastoral romances was well established. Since Theodotion lived and worked in Alexandria at a crucial meeting point of Jewish and Hellenistic culture it is not surprising that he produced a Hellenized version of the Susanna story.[8]

Martin Braun describes "subjects of erotic interest...[as the] subject matter *par excellence* of ancient novels and short stories." (1938:44-45). Braun understands why the romance version of Susanna would be preferred by the Christian patriarchs for inclusion in their canon: they come, he claims, from an oriental culture that has to learn to accommodate itself to the conquering Hellenic city culture.

> In its wake had come courtesanship and a certain general tendency to eroticism in the manner of living. It is precisely in the severity and violence of the polemic against eroticism and courtesanship that the strength of these social phenomena can be perceived... We hear the voice of a society that feels itself

---

[7] I can think of one exception. There is a Lotto painting in which the bath is in the foreground and the judgment in the back. I have seen Daniel in only one drawing - a Rembrandt. There is a painting of *Susanna and the Elders* by a woman, Artemisia Gentileschi. Mary Garrard (1982) has written about the picture at length, and about its relationship to the painter's own life, specifically her experience of rape.

[8] The history of the translations is not clear. The *Encyclopedia Judaica* says that "the Theodotion version of Daniel is given by practically all the Septuagint manuscripts with the exception of the Alexandrian" (IV.855). For a while it was assumed that Theodotion was merely rewriting a text he found in Greek. It has also been argued, however, that he was working from more than one semitic original (either Hebrew or Aramaic or both) now lost. See Moore, ed. (1977).

most seriously threatened by Eros: already it is beginning to regard love as the mightiest weapon of sin wielded by the evil spirit Beliar. This heralds, though as yet from a great distance, the painful conflict of the human spirit in late antiquity, when men and women, terrorized by the demon of sensuality, took refuge in penitence, asceticism and monastic life. (45)

Braun does not notice, however, how frequently in Greek literature the erotic is embedded in the pastoral, as it is in the case of the Susanna story. In pastoral, as will become clear, the relationship to Eros is different, is in fact, entirely ambivalent. It is, in fact, exactly that mix of voyeurism and vision that Steiner describes as characteristic of romance.

Four separate conditions of pastoral romance can be identified in the Theodotion version of the Susanna story. First, it plays, as all pastorals do, on the motif of the sophisticate in the country. The Elders, judges, no less, citified sophisticates, are found lurking in the garden like satyrs. All their knowledge and probity is on vacation - they are reduced to basic passions. In the Greek tradition, there is an ambiguity about the satyr and his lust: sometimes they are darkly evil, sometimes comic. He is a threat to the innocence of country life, but as pure unaccommodated lust he is also a natural part of it. He rarely triumphs, as he doesn't here. The Old Lecher, however, is figured by the pastoral as unambiguously unnatural. Sex and passion are for the young - period. Old people are married, and neither romance nor pastoral is very interested in sexuality within marriage. In *Susanna*, as in the Greek pastoral, then, (e.g., Longus' *Daphnis and Chloe*), unruly sexuality threatens innocence, but sexuality itself is not ipso facto evil. There is a legitimate and fitting sexual partner for Susanna, namely her husband. She is expected to be chaste, but not virginal. In the apocryphal texts, the Elders are repeatedly censored not for their lechery but for their having allowed their lust to corrupt their responsibility as judges. "And they perverted their own mind, and turned about their eyes that they might not look unto heaven, nor remember just judgments." We learn that this is not the first time the judges have threatened women with abuse of power if they did not submit. Daniel lectures them: "Beauty hath deceived thee, and lust hath perverted thine heart. Thus have ye dealt with the daughters of Israel, and they for fear companied with you."

The second pastoral motif in the story is that of the woman in the landscape - more precisely, the woman as part of the landscape, part of nature. The analogy between the water, seeds, fertility and fruitfulness of a landscape and human sexuality is evidenced in the earliest poetry. In a discussion of gardens and ekphrasis of gardens in Greek Byzantine romances, A.R. Littlewood takes the all but obvious next step by asserting that because of the analogy between human and natural fertility, "a garden, in itself unnecessary to the plot or argument, is not unlikely to be invested with erotic undertones.... Frequently the garden is the scene for erotic action." (1979:97) In pastoral, the escape to the country or, in miniature, to a garden provides rest, healing, and pleasure. The shepherd gathers fruit from trees that need no cultivation, drinks milk from his flock, bathes in rippling streams or forest lakes, and watches beautiful women do the same. Littlewood notes that in the classical sources, gardens are connected more closely to heroines than to heroes. "The garden is a part, and usually the most important part, of the heroine's original and personal setting." (99) Young shepherds and shepherdesses both learn about sex by imitating the animals they tend. But within the leveling agenda of the pastoral, according to which there is no private property and the gifts of nature belong to everyone, the stronger identity of women with nature overwhelms whatever equality she might otherwise have; like sunshine and figs, she is available to the young man for the taking, and with no more guilt than is involved in the plucking of a ripe fruit. Then, in the golden age of humankind which the excursion to the country mimics, sex was no sin. There, as we learn in Tasso's *Aminta, s'ei piace è lice* - Whatever pleases is legitimate.

The Greek romance is a locus classicus of the motif of the enclosed garden, the *hortus conclusus*, which it borrows from the *Song of Songs*, and which was later developed by Christian allegorists into a figure of the Virgin Mary. The enclosed garden preserves a small part of nature's pleasures for the holder of the key. The woman, of course, is not only within the garden, she is herself the garden of her lover's pleasure. The woman has no public role or voice. The garden, thus, shares in the significance of bodies: like the pastoral scene as a whole it is sensuous and immediate. This motif overlaps with the one above, but adds another dimension. The woman is not only a natural object, not only a possession, but is fixed and hedged in. She has neither freedom of movement nor of expression. She lives, and in fact the whole story takes place, in a world of limited horizons, private enclosures. For Bryan Reardon, "the narrative [of the Greek romances] expresses a social and personal myth, of the private individual isolated and insecure in a world too big for him, and finding his security, his very identity, in love." (28-29)

The fourth pastoral motif in the Theodotion Susanna is its plot structure and its resolution by means of rhetorical *anagnorisis*. The plot is fueled by the imbalance of power between the main characters described above, and the Elder's attempt to take advantage of their judicial power. Vengeance is, of course, God's. Reardon notes that the participation of the gods is typical of Greek romance. Their struggles keep the plot going for while, but eventually the hero's salvation results from divine benevolence of which *peripeteia* and *anagnorisis* are the signs. (1991:25) Deception is always cleared up by the *deus ex machina*, the oracle that saves the day. Within a moment we move from lie to truth, from darkness to revelation. Terence Cave considers *anagnorisis* to be "the signature or synecdoche for fiction as a whole" (1988:255), flouting, as it does, the vraisemblance governed by everyday epistemological rules. Enmeshed in a web of deception which might produce tragedy, the romance produces the knowledge needed to get the situation back on track, and always in the nick of time. And if we needed any further evidence that the narrative details of the events in Babylon are being manipulated to make a good story,

Pervo (1991:148fn) notes that Daniel waits with his revelation until after the false judgment is given.

Bakhtin (1981:95) notes of Greek romances that because all their adventures right up to their happy endings are controlled by chance and coincidence, experience and analysis are useless. The prophet Daniel's testimony could not have been predicted. Yet his appearance is not coincidental. Daniel is a conduit for truth, an oracle, responding to Susanna's need by declaring the judges to be slanderers. His youth aligns him with the fools and children in folklore whose innocence and ignorance is successful as a hermeneutic, where (again) the normal adult ways of knowing have failed to uncover the truth. There is an additional irony in their defeat at the hands of a young man, after their slanderous tale of seeing but not being able to "hold" the young man they "saw" with Susanna. Their testimony, even as slander, has an element of truth: indeed, they were not strong enough, as they say, to do what they wanted to do. Strength and youth, however, in this moral romance, are employed on behalf of virtue and truth, not for the advancement of perversion. Cave notes (488) that because *anagnorisis* mocks standard epistemological method, it weakens its claim to be a satisfying truth at the very moment it makes that claim. If, like so much else in romance, it is produced only by coincidence or chance, it might very well not have occurred. But the ending of the tale is not pure romance. After he has spoken as a prophet, a mouthpiece of God, Daniel turns to the worldly job the Elders turned away from, namely, securing the procedures of ascertaining truth and advancing justice.[9]

This brief summary of the crucial pastoral conditions in Theodotion's version of Susanna makes clear that the painters had a textual basis for their pastoral settings for Susanna; with one interesting and important exception. The text itself, the Theodotion text, that is, the one with all the pastoral characteristics enumerated above, lacks one fundamental detail that the painters provided. It does not describe Susanna as ever actually taking a bath. Therefore, of course, it doesn't tell us that the elders saw her naked.

> So it was that while they were watching closely for the opportune day, she came in [to the garden] as usual, accompanied only by two maids. And she wanted to bathe in the garden as it was very hot. Since no one was there except the two elders who had hidden themselves and were spying on her, she said to her maids, "Bring me oil and cosmetics, and close the garden gates so I can bathe. So they did as she had ordered: they closed the garden gates and went out by the side doors to get the things she had asked them for; they did

---

[9] Beyond his youth, there is another oddity in casting Daniel in the role of oracle, and that is that he is not considered by rabbinic commentators to be a prophet. His performance as such is just the kind of behavior, like miracle working, that was becoming increasingly distrusted as the distance from the age of prophecy grew, and the institutions of law took its place (M. Vigoda, oral communication).

not see the elders because they were hidden. As soon as the maids had left,
the two elders got up and accosted her.
"Look!" they said, "the garden gates are shut, and nobody can see us;
and we desire you. So let us have you. If not, we will testify against you,
saying that a young man was with you, and that is why you had dismissed
your maids from thee." (Moore, ed. 94)

The bathing scene, it seems, is imagined. It is the painterly parallel of
Susanna's own desire to bathe in the heat of the day, and the Elders' wish-
fulfillment slander. The story spoke clearly to them of the enjoyment of a
woman's body, of the lust of the eyes, and they represented it as they saw it in
the mind's eye. The genre of the text and the verb "bathe" (twice) apparently
carried greater semantic weight than the grammar, in which the bath is
something only wanted and anticipated. The editor of the *Anchor Bible* is
equally fooled: "The bath scene (sic) in Theodotion", he tells us, is "a later
addition. If so, from a literary point of view it is a most welcome one: the
bathing scene not only excites the elders, thereby enabling them to attempt their
dastardly deed, but it can also fire the imagination of some readers. Of such
considerations are good stories made!" (97,fn. 15) If excitement is your aim,
then truth (even to the text in front of you - I do not speak of truth to any
anterior historical situation) or ethics remains secondary.[10]

The Jewish text which the Theodotion story replaced, however, that is,
the Old Greek Septuagint text, has other fish to fry. It is not interested in
private worlds, but rather with the community's need for just judges. The
account of the apocryphal Susanna story in the 1911 edition of the *Encyclopedia
Britannica* gets the emphasis right, if perhaps concealing the hypothetical nature
of its assertion: proposing its composition in about 100-90 B.C.E. "When
Simon Ben Shitah was president of the Sanhedrin, its object was to support the
attempts of the Pharisees to bring about a reform in the administration of the
law courts."[11] The first line of the text as we have it is about the wickedness
of the judges,[12] and the whole first section of the poem is about the connivance

---

[10] Martin Braun makes the same mistake. He says, "In contrast to the older Septuagint
version, in which the two elders approach Susanna, who is walking in her garden, and try
to violate her, the situation in the more recent version has been so rearranged that they spy
upon her, while she is bathing in the deserted park" (96).

[11] This date is an educated guess by Robert Henry Charles, author of the *Encyclopedia
Britannica* article (1911: Vol.VII, 807). Moore is more cautious: "Perhaps the one
incontestable generalization" about the Greek additions to Daniel is that they were made after
the rabbinic canonization of the text in the second century C.E. (24). Their composition,
however, was of course, earlier than their inclusion. Moore sets c. 100 B.C.E. as the
terminus ad quem for the composition of Susanna, although its original may be in much
earlier folklore (29).

[12] In the *Anchor Bible*, ed. Moore, the first line is assumed to be only the first surviving
line, and is thus numbered 5b for two good reasons. First, the line itself appears in the
expanded text of Theodotion, as line 5b; second, the deictic "of such" indicates that the

of the corrupt judges against Susanna.

The focus of the story here is on the sexual corruption of the elders which is seen as the cause of their slander and misuse of the legal system to condemn the innocent and protect the wicked. The turning point comes when Susanna prays. God hears her prayer (1.35) and responds by inspiring Daniel with a prophetic vision. The youth condemns their judicial practice and undoes the damage of the mistrial by the legal strategy of examining the witnesses separately, thereby proving that their imaginations, and not Susanna's actions, underwrote their testimony.

Like the Theodotion, the Old Greek text has no bath, nor any mention of a projected bath. It has no maids whose temporary dismissal the judges take advantage of. Susanna appears naked only at her trial, and there it is not for her own satisfaction, as it is in the paintings, but at the order of the judges, who thus in part, at least, satisfy their lust. That her nakedness is a humiliation to her is clear; it provokes her tears and the tears of those who love her. We cannot know, with the information currently at hand, whether the older text was innocent of the Greek tradition of pastoral romance, or if it rejected it. We can, however, see the earlier text to be offering a legal procedure as a protection against the machinations of slander, the miscarriage of justice, and the victimization of an innocent. Its own ambiguity is that it still witnesses a need to vouchsafe civil procedure or reform by the prophetic voice of Daniel whose name indeed means God is my judge. In the absence of oracles and prophets, however, the law remains to protect Susanna - to pull her out of the water, so to speak.

The older text sees the perversion of justice as dangerous, but the Theodotion misses the point. That text allows the interpretations that are indeed read off it for at least another sixteen hundred years, in the tradition of Western art and literature. Instead of teaching the necessity of civic justice, we learn once again that women are dangerously enchanting. More broadly, in the pastoral text and paintings, the insistence on the use of intelligence in ethical life is rejected. This is a fundamentally skeptical position, in that it breaks the connection between reason and behavior. As such, it is not only a rejection of the Jewish tradition, but of the Platonic, metaphysical tradition as well.

That the Jewish tradition rejected the seduction of beauty held out by the Hellenistic world has been argued in several places by Harold Fisch (1988 and 1993). Furthermore, in the period of the codification of the Talmud, the rabbis struggled to close the books on prophecy, magic, and miracles. The weight of

---

words that follow are meant to describe some people already referred to. We do not, however, have any right to assume that the lost lines are exactly the same as the first verses of Theodotion ("There dwelt a man in Babylon..."). On the contrary, we have a reason to assume that they were not since the information about Susanna and her family that is given in the first 4 lines of the Theodotion is provided later, in line 7, of the earlier text. The earlier text, then, may have begun with only one line before the existing one, and that one specifying that two ancients of the people had been appointed judges.

rabbinic authority came down solidly behind law and getting on with the struggles of daily life. There is a strange story in the Babylonian Talmud with which I would like to end my paper.

> Once Rabbi Jose of Yokereth had day-labourers [working] in the field; night set in and no food was brought to them and they said to his son, 'We are hungry'. Now they were resting under a fig tree and he exclaimed: Fig tree, fig tree, bring forth thy fruit that my father's labourers may eat. It brought forth fruit and they ate. Meanwhile the father came and said to them, Do not bear a grievance against me; the reason for my delay is because I have been occupied up till now on an errand of charity. The labourers replied, May God satisfy you even as your son has satisfied us. Whereupon he asked: Whence? And they told him what had happened. Thereupon he said to his son: My son, you have troubled your Creator to cause the fig tree to bring forth its fruits before its time, may you too be taken hence before your time! (*Ta'anith*, 24a)

What needs explaining here is why the father should pronounce so harsh a curse upon his son; why is he not grateful to his son for fulfilling the duty of feeding the workers when the father himself was not able to perform it? The son, it seems, did the right thing, but in the wrong way. Surely right to see his obligation to feed the workers, the son should have taken the example of Abraham who greeted the angels by preparing food in the normal household way: "And Abraham ran to the herd, and fetched a calf tender and good...and he hurried to prepare it. And he took butter and milk and the calf which he had dressed, and set it before them." (Gen. 18) The story teaches the anti-pastoral lesson: we are not to depend on miraculous fig trees, or on young prophets popping up to save us from our missteps. We are bidden to depend on intelligence and law, and to resist the seduction of beauty.

Hosannas to an American Susanna
Sharon Deykin Baris
Bar-Ilan University

It took a Connecticut Yankee poet, both inventive and alert to moments of individual crisis, to demonstrate how Americans have long resisted peering at Susanna in ways that replicate the Elders' leering gaze, and to suggest why he and others would instead join their voices with hers, singing hosannas in her praise. Wallace Stevens' 1921 poem "Peter Quince at the Clavier" evokes Susanna's beauty, that is true; but its dynamics go further, to acknowledge and even celebrate her response to a threatened assault, as the narrative is presented in the apocryphal Susanna and the Elders.[1] In a poetic rendition of Susanna's story, Stevens continues certain vital actions that Susanna herself had long ago begun.

Whereas European paintings of Susanna are said to repeat the Elders' lustful and delimiting gaze by making this young woman seem only an object in a viewing process that is in turn extended to the viewer who looks at such renditions,[2] Wallace Stevens and other American writers, musicians and artists,

---

[1] The text used in this discussion is *The Book of Susanna* (N.Y.: Anchor, 1974). All citations within the text are to this edition, given in parentheses.

[2] Mary Ann Caws, for example, shows how *Susanna* paintings emphasize "our obsession with the act of framing and representation as such," *The Art of Interference: Stressed Readings in Verbal & Visual Texts* (Princeton: Princeton Univ. Press, 1989), 218. Mieke Bal's section on "Susanna and the Viewer" begins with a similar assumption: "It seems obvious that the story of Susanna, in whatever 'version,' thematizes the position of the viewer,'" since as she puts it, "In a sense, the story of Susanna is about illegitimate viewing," *Reading Rembrandt: Beyond the Word-Image Opposition* (Cambridge: Cambridge Univ. Press, 1991), 161-176. Bal makes the important observation, however, that Susanna paintings invoke both words and images, and can be read with "reference to a verbal--philosophical as well as practical, ideological, and political--discussion going on in the society that generated the work," 45. It is against such a background, indeed, that my study can be placed as a discussion of certain philosophical, ideological, and humane senses within American hosannas to Susanna.

119

I will show, most characteristically take note of Susanna's subjective and outspoken response. To them she is a lively figure who vigorously declares her own central role in the story's unfolding. Americans' many acknowledgments of Susanna's voice and of her function in speaking out in the story of Susanna and the Elders can be traced in a wide range of literary and artistic works from the early nineteenth century until today. In them this woman's bold action is exemplary. The importance of Susanna's resistance to forces of collusion and conformity might indeed be recognized by cultural historians now more than ever, as Americans seek to emphasize multi-vocal and plural expressions of national culture. A study of her function in the story may serve as a basis for understanding a wide range of personal voices that have long been raised, shaping a vital and significant national tradition.

The name of Susanna, foregrounded in so many famous European paintings known as *Susanna and the Elders*, has only to a very limited extent been used in the titles of American works. It does provide the heading and blithe refrain, for example, of the 1847 Stephen Foster song, "Oh, Susanna!", and the name of a far darker opera, Carlisle Floyd's *Susannah* written a century later; it was also used for Thomas Hart Benton's social-realist painting of the 1930s, *Susanna and the Elders*. More often, however, Susanna has played her significant part in American works that would not seem to be telling her story. Her important voice can be heard, as I will demonstrate, in such prominent tales and novels as Nathaniel Hawthorne's "Rappaccini's Daughter" and *The Scarlet Letter*, in *The Portrait of a Lady* by Henry James, and in *The Book of Daniel* by E.L. Doctorow, as well as in Stevens' "Peter Quince at the Clavier." Outlines of her story appear in recent texts by Eudora Welty and Saul Bellow, and its implications are notable in productions including Tennessee Williams' *Glass Menagerie*, Alfred Hitchcock's film, *Rear Window*, or in Garry Marshall's 1992 film, *Frankie and Johnny*. Attracted to Susanna's story, Americans have repeatedly chosen to join their voice with hers as a national art form. Singing along with Susanna might well be termed a most American--or even post-American--custom, one that is long and wide, if not fully measured or understood.

Imagining Susanna's story from her vantage, one could say that the action begins with her own voice, first heard in her confident directions to her two servants, and then sounded in her loud declaration in response to an assault made upon her privacy with the Elders' intrusion into her garden. In support of such an emphasis upon voices and not merely others' looking at her, it is interesting to note that what happens next is also described in terms of declarations made to her. For the Elders state their propositions as kinds of narrative options Susanna herself might choose. They suggest harsh tellings of her life story: "Give us your consent, and lie with us. If you refuse, we will bear witness against you" (Sus 20-21). Part and parcel of their shocking attack is their demand for submission to their narratives: either to share their conspiracy (to "lie with us" in both the physical and moral senses of that phrase) or to suffer public defamation ("witness against thee"). What Susanna so brilliantly recognizes is that there is no hope of safety in making a choice between the plots they offer. For indeed there is none. Their collusion is evident, as she inwardly murmurs, "I am straitened on every side." Their conspiratorial project itself threatens her, starkly denying as it does, any means of maintaining her own versions--in her enclosed garden or elsewhere. The straits or constraints she faces, then, are between her desire to maintain some private story--which, like her garden, would but allow for their collusive threats--and exposure to the wider arenas of multiple and variant renditions. It is upon recognizing such constraints that Susanna speaks out.

Crucially, Susanna does not offer a single version to counter the Elders. Her response is the very act of raising "a loud voice"--a phrase that is used four times in this story (Sus 24; 42; 46; 60).[3] It is in her powerful voice personally raised in one terrible crisis, that Susanna insists that the possibility of particular versions--hers and others'--itself remain open. That is what she is voicing so very loud and clear. And that is the message which Daniel and the townspeople--and those who recognize Susanna's role in this apocryphal story--will finally come to acknowledge.

To that end, Wallace Stevens in "Peter Quince at the Clavier" creates his poetic response to Susanna's voice. Stevens' poetic rendition of her story follows Susanna's example by evoking still further versions, as his artistry so richly shows. Introducing her, Stevens uses a title that places another focalizing artist-figure, Peter Quince, at a baroque keyboard, poised and readied for a performance. But before Peter Quince begins his action, or before this poem commences, Peter Quince's name itself invokes the idea of variations and renditions. It hints at an intertextual recycling not only of this name, but of similar actions of version-making in Shakespeare's *A Midsummer Night's Dream*, in which a character named Peter Quince shows his penchant for improvising on traditional props and staging while figuring, or "disfiguring" as he puts it, his own production. Stevens' title thus is a complex initiation into the possibility of further figurations, which indeed then follow. They are the many "imaginings" of Susanna that her story induces.[4]

In describing his subject Quince then shifts registers, drawing upon still other media in the process. For it "is music" that arouses this artist (the poem punningly says that a "strain" is "waked") about Susanna. When Stevens' Peter Quince plays out his renditions on the keyboard of a clavier, he plays upon the possibilities of the baroque musical instrument, itself known for the performance

---

[3] In most of the translations of this story that I have examined, the text repeats the centrally important word or phrase concerning a "raised voice," or "loud voice" or "loudly spoken," drawn from the same Greek terms repeatedly used in the Septuagint. The basic version to which I refer is the Theodotion text, the version used in most American texts and biblical encyclopedias; any other references will be noted.

[4] Wallace Stevens, "Peter Quince at the Clavier," *Collected Poems of Wallace Stevens* (New York: Knopf, 1954), 89-92.

of variations. A clavier was used, traditionally, for achieving an effect or process known as the realization of a figured bass line. In such realizations, a clavier was combined with other instruments (like the winds, or basses, horns, or viols--all mentioned in the poem), to allow an obligato voice to sing out above a spare counterpart below, while the rich middle ground was filled in by the improvisations of a harpsichordist according to the harmonic numbers, or figures, indicated above the bass line of the score.[5] Such notations were thus to be realized--variously and often brilliantly--in virtuoso performances by keyboard artists such as Stevens' Peter Quince.

Very different figures in Stevens' poem suggest still another range of expressions, as when Susanna's "blue-shadowed silk," and the springs of her "devotions" as she sits at a "bank" beside the water of her "still garden" form a pattern to be noticed. These details invoke other well-known configurations, typical of medieval enclosed garden paintings in which Susanna was often portrayed. These figurings, too, increase a sense of her multiple renditions as they are often traced in pictorial or iconic representations of Susanna.[6] Stevens' use of several registers--of theater, music, and visual art--in each case promotes an awareness of improvisations, or realizations, or variations, characteristic to these media, even as Peter Quince or Stevens' "Peter Quince at the Clavier" suggests so many versions of Susanna.

With the text's first words: "Just as," so we, in turn, continue responding to the Susanna story over the duration of our reading. We also, in the other comparative sense of that phrase, match possible readings or variations one against another in recognitions of both our own and Susanna's lively potential. If such a redoubled sense of the first words is shown in ongoing as well as responsive reactions, it constitutes the very means of "thinking of" Susanna; and that action itself is important. For a willing participation in the poem's multiple possibilities would undo any single or Elder-like telling of her story--or of our reading of it.

Susanna's voice could be the very sign and signal for other impassioned outbursts. Her voice, in the apocryphal text, draws attention to the powers of her carnal presence. That is appropriate, since in her power of speech she demonstrates that her particular body is the ground for making her own personal and passional claims, in deflection of their single-minded lust ("we are burning with desire for thee"). Her outspokenness also attests to her potential for using the diverse means of language in framing still other stories. That, too, is

---

[5] For a discussion of realization in this poem, see Kinereth Meyer and Sharon Baris, "Reading the Score of 'Peter Quince at the Clavier': Stevens, Music, and the Visual Arts," *Wallace Stevens Journal* 12 (1988):56-67. Stevens' record collection contained many examples of baroque works, as a list would show. See Michael O. Stegman, "Wallace Stevens and Music: A Discography of Stevens' Record Collection," *Wallace Stevens Journal* 3 (1979):79-97.

[6] Alfred L. Kellogg shows the linking of Susanna and the *hortus conclusus* tradition, in "Susanna and the Merchant's Tale," *Speculum* XXXV (1960):275.

suitable, since it is her very different voice that disrupts this scene. It is the possibility of separate bodies and places, and of distinctive versions--both implicit in Susanna's raised voice--that will be used to challenge the collusion these men threaten ("we will bear witness against thee"), when Daniel's judgment reveals the physical and verbal discrepancies of their testimony.

All expressions of Susanna might be said to be inherently multiple, variously "of" the ancient apocryphal story (which is in fact known today in translations and variant texts[7]); it may be the intrinsic variability within those texts we have that is so appropriately heightened by renditions considering Susanna's own insistence upon versions. The focus of this apocryphal book itself, moreover, is divided or diffuse: although it is Susanna who rejects the forces of collusion in her garden and in the world, the story thereafter takes a sudden turn away from her wise perspective and toward the feats of Daniel, when he so famously comes to judgment. And while the text emphasizes the fact of his "young youth" as if to promise some fresh or independent views, the story equally points out that Daniel's wisdom derives from heavenly sources (in the Septuagint it is an angel, in the Theodotion version it is the Lord who inspires him). Such a divine authorization of Daniel, more oddly still, then serves to support the mere possibility of seeing multiple versions as the sum and substance of Daniel's astounding insight! What is that, in turn, but the reinforcement of Susanna's outcry against any single (whether collusive or authorized) version? So Daniel's judgment, after all, becomes a variation upon the wisdom that has already been heard in Susanna's abjuring voice.

A most striking feature of Susanna and the Elders is, indeed, the way that Susanna in her crucial garden scene and again in her public trial establishes the terms for all that follows. Her own example is reenacted in the language used when Daniel comes to judgment. When Daniel speaks before the town, he does so, we are told, "with a loud voice" (Sus 46; emphasis added). The text's identical iteration in describing Susanna's outspoken cries and Daniel's interjection emphasizes a parallel between them, as if in structural recognition of her impact upon him and in turn upon the story's outcome. Just as Susanna's raised voice rejects cooption, so Daniel's recognition of the presence of disparity between the Elders' testimonies constitutes his judgment against them. Driving apart their statements, that is, Daniel makes public policy of Susanna's outspoken performance, he is but encoding her declaration. Her voicing is her refusal to hide a recognition of separate presences and their independent views. Susanna's wise insight is her judgment of true dissent.

It is interesting to note that Daniel, too, takes advantage of a doubleness

---

[7] There are two versions of the no longer extant "Semitic original" of the Susanna story. It was, according to traditional commentary, located at or adjacent to Chapter 13 of the Book of Daniel. See the introduction to "*Susanna*: Chapter 13 of the Greek Version of Daniel" *The New Oxford Annotated Bible With the Apocryphal/Deuterocanonical Books*, ed. Bruce M. Metzger, and Roland E. Murphy (New York: Oxford Univ. Press, 1991), 179.

implicit within the physical act of voicing, as he develops his legal case for her. He uses the sensual possibilities within language, of word-play itself, both to sunder the Elders' collusion and to declare their punishment. When Daniel talks to these conspirators about "cutting thee in two," his brilliant use of language beautifully suits and counters these Elders' crime. In some translations of Susanna and the Elders the trees named by the conspirators while under Daniel's cross-examination are given as a "yew tree" for one Elder and a "clove tree" for the other. So when Daniel hears their conflicting evidence as proof of their lying, he can use their very words to speak of "hewing" and "cleaving" their attempted collusions apart.[8] In the act of condemning them, Daniel insists upon various sensual means to contradict and countermand their lustful forcing of a conspiracy upon Susanna. By using terms that are sensible, and variant, hence riven, Daniel is indeed rendering judgments.

At the end of Susanna and the Elders the townsfolk receive Daniel's view. Unlike some chorus of consent, they do not validate its truth in any single version as the outcome. The text emphasizes how they, too, have learned the message of Susanna's raised voice. "With that," the text concludes, "all the assembly cried out with a loud voice" (emphasis added). In a final iteration of this same phrase, the assembly signifies its dawning recognition of the profound personal and communal implications of the story of Susanna. The significance of such a scene of shared understanding might well span outward with far-reaching social and cultural implications toward those who would celebrate Susanna in America. Her story would be reenacted in persistent, sometimes subtle, often colorful attention to such a communal outcome, as--or "just as"-- many Americans joined their voice with hers in repeated celebrations.

For Susanna's raised voice in all its compound physical and narrative personal potentialities provides an evocative model for questioning the implications of a single, exceptionalist, or consensual concept of American selfhood. The act of singing along with Susanna as a claim for raising one's voice against monolithic forces could well be performed in anthems of many verses. Imagining Susanna neither as a reified object of others' spying (as so often shown in the Tintoretto painting[9]), nor even as the means of furthering an abstractly held ideal (as if to promote some singular American dream[10]),

---

[8] On wordplay and the way it often is maintained even in translations, see *Oxford Annotated Bible*, "Susanna," 181, n.54-59.

[9] Speaking of the viewer's response to Tintoretto's *Susanna and the Elders*, Caws comments that "our own spying is a good part of the deal," 263. Caws goes on to state that Stevens "captures just this secret watching," a reading to which my sense of Stevens' dynamics of musical and artistic realization stands opposed.

[10] Annette Kolodny demonstrates the flattening nature of an imaginary construct as American national myth; it is an ideal that "effaces diversity" in the name of continuities. Her title is self-explanatory: "Letting Go Our Grand Obsessions: Notes Toward a New Literary History of the American Frontiers," *American Literature* 64 (1991):2-3, 13. The fullest exposition of such an American idealist myth, its premises and consequences, is

Americans throughout their history might rather have heeded this woman's cry. With its heartfelt call for bespeaking many carnal recognitions, it would alert them to other personal and independent claims, as well.

It was Emerson, writing in the 1840s, who advocated such understandings among his fellow Americans, in contrast to more widespread but small-minded habits of thinking that he called a kind of national "foolish consistency."[11] In an essay titled "Self-Reliance" Emerson praised personal outspokenness, itself, as he rebuked a society "that everywhere is in conspiracy." Calling for an expression of self-reliance that is, as he put it, conformity's "aversion," Emerson might even have had the intrusive Elders in mind when he urged Americans never to "peep or steal or skulk up and down with the air of...an interloper" in America's lands and gardens (149; 155). Imagining a different enclosed garden landscape for his country, Emerson declared that when we "walk on our own feet...work with our own hands...speak our own minds," then a nation "will for the first time exist," based upon "the dread of man and the love of man" as both a "wall of defence and a wreath of joy" ("Divinity School Address" 79-80). Like an artistic Peter Quince who could transpose Susanna's exotic Babylonian setting into the "tambourines" and "Byzantines" of Stevens' poem, Emerson in his essays repeatedly reimagines familiar settings, as if better to appreciate Susanna's challenge in such environs. So he punningly plays on new hopes as against Old World collusions in fallen empires. As if to evoke the Levantine atmosphere of Susanna's story, he invites his countrymen to "dilate and conspire" with him in a "dawn" that is "my Assyria" ("Nature" 27). Replacing that ancient repressive empire with a "more illustrious monarchy," Emerson hints even at a Susanna-like sense of being straitened anywhere but in the "unbounded, unboundable empire" of independent nonconformism. He deems the "private life of one individual" to be better "than any kingdom in history" ("American Scholar" 76).

Emerson's struggle against consensus, however, was not only a personal or political cry, but also carried far wider social and philosophical implications, as the American philosopher Stanley Cavell recently has shown. Giving voice to what he assesses to be a tradition of philosophy that follows Emerson's claim for self-reliance as the "aversion" of conformity as a kind of national conspiracy, Cavell sees Emersonian aversiveness to be a founding, or a constitutional, American dynamic.[12] Averse to conformity even to some supposedly abstract ideal, or to a principle of idealism itself, it works, instead,

---

presented in Sacvan Bercovitch, *The Puritan Origins of the American Self* (New Haven: Yale Univ. Press, 1975).

[11] Ralph Waldo Emerson, *Selections from Ralph Waldo Emerson*, ed. Stephen E. Whicher (Boston: Houghton Mifflin, 1957), 149. Further references to Emerson's essays are to this volume.

[12] Emerson as the founder of a tradition of American philosophy, is propounded by Stanley Cavell, *Conditions Handsome and Unhandsome: The Constitution of Emersonian Perfectionism* (Chicago: Univ. of Chicago Press, 1990).

toward a recognition of many ordinary and human voices, as each citizen's worthy act of national and personal responsibility. And it is within such a fundamental American philosophy stated by Emerson and understood by Cavell, I believe, that Susanna's story has been so appealing. Her example resonates within American art and literature as an ethics of declaring and of heeding individual voices. As such it is the very statement and the impetus for a certain kind of New World thinking, one that bespeaks Americans' great praising, along with that of Susanna.

Her voice had been heard in America long before Stevens' time, from colonial days onward. It served not only as a basis for lofty Emersonian lectures, but did its work, as well, in Americans' daily lives as settlers and citizens settled their land, or sought greater fortunes in moving westward. For Americans seemed to trust, yet inwardly question, an encompassing national myth that had been spreading through their land, threatening to possess it. This was the dream of an American exceptionalist future, based upon a preordained and overarching typological "plot" as a vision or narrative to be achieved within its bounds.[13] A sense of America as the "New World" conveyed not only a belief in material progress, but also a hoped-for spiritual condition in which the sins of a fallen past would be regenerated, in that corrective sense of new, as well.

Some American settlers, to be sure, derived sustenance for their efforts from passages of other-worldly phraseology in the Bible, as when the Book of Isaiah's poetical prophecies seemed to promise one peaceful day in which lions and lambs would dwell together. But other Americans, at the same time, found such blithe promises and texts, or Edward Hicks' famous mid-century series of paintings entitled "Peaceable Kingdom" based upon them, to be strangely benign and far too passive for any use as a basis for pursuing difficult and even deeply troubled new ways.[14] If such citizens sought another scriptural source, they might have turned, accordingly, to the biblical Book of Daniel, with its more dynamic, even disruptive, prophecies as the foretelling of an American future; for that book, too, promised an End of Days. It was widely cited, moreover, for the purposes of predicting the timing of the years and days before the very End, especially so in increasingly difficult times during a period of national

---

[13] Thomas Shepard, for example, spoke of "God's main plot," or "God's deep plot," for America's future. Shepard's daily views, in his extensive diaries, are published under a similar title, *God's Great Plot: The Paradoxes of Puritan Piety*, ed. Michael McGiffert (Amherst: Univ. of Massachusetts Press, 1972), 119, 141.

[14] Edward Hicks' several paintings of a "peaceable kingdom," however idealized or sincere, can indeed provide ironic comment upon an abstract concept of destiny. For in them the heroic action of Penn and the Indians is oddly remote and obscure--barely visible in the distance of these paintings--while the only human eyes foregrounded are located in the animals' baleful stares. Any woman's figure, if present, is infantilized. Would not such depersonalized, undifferentiated and ungendered scenes of non-action in these works convey a sense of the repressions implicit in such an imagined--hardly peaceable--reign?

strife as the millennial epoch then seemed upon them.[15]

Daniel's colorful personality itself was worthy. That old-time Puritan preacher Roger Williams, referring to Daniel and "the three famous Jewes [who were] cast into the fiery furnace for refusing to fall down in a non-conformity to the whole conforming world (Dan.3:21)..." most typically challenged his countrymen to emulate Daniel: "Truth... God's people were and ought to be Nonconformitants."[16] Well-known hymns would challenge, "Dare to be a Daniel," even as their refrains further explained this reference both as "Dare to stand alone," and "Dare to make it known." But if the biblical Daniel was bold in predicting Americans' futures, the Book of Daniel as a whole was also more deeply troubling, in the implications such visions contained. While scriptural commentators on the Book of Daniel, from the time of the earliest rabbis and through the subsequent exegesis of church fathers such as Jerome and others, had noted a general westward-moving redemptive tendency in this text, it was the American Puritan interpreters who saw in the Book of Daniel a particular relevance--for better or for worse--to the actual settlers of the New World.[17] Jonathan Edwards may have noted such real geographic and historic facts, in their timely juxtaposition, to be God's way of "doing some great thing to make way for the introduction of [glory that is] to take its rise from the new world."[18] He found deep fascination in the relentless paths of kingdoms; but others sensed lurking dangers therein, as well. Here, too, the Book of Daniel and the actions of its eponymous hero could seem appropriate--painfully so--to these perplexed Americans.

Deep uncertainties are evinced in Daniel's own reactions to his views, when he is repeatedly described as "severely distressed"; "overcome and sick for some days," he is often "pale" and "trembling" (Dan. 4:19, 8:27, 10:8-11). Daniel's fears are not caused by the king or by any moments of intense

---

[15] The two earliest American sermons published in the 1640s were on the Book of Daniel. See J.F.Maclear, "New England and the Fifth Monarchy: The Quest for Millennium in Early American Puritanism," *William and Mary Quarterly* 32 (1975):223-60. The later sermons of the Millerites, furthermore, drew upon Daniel's many references to the "time appointed" or "seventy weeks" and the "half of the week" and so on, with increasing intensity as the end of the 19th century, or presumably the time of the end, drew near.

[16] See Roger Williams, "The Bloudy Tenet of Persecution," in *The Puritans*, Vol I, ed. Perry Miller, and Thomas Johnson (1938, reprint, New York: Harper & Row, 1963), 220.

[17] Sacvan Bercovitch emphasizes the typological interpretive measures according to which Americans foretold their nation's ideal future as a "kingdom of the latter days," and notes the importance of the biblical Book of Daniel. Bercovitch explains the links between prophetic texts and a sense of an inevitable course of history, drawing links between a presumed "course of empire" and Americans' sense of destiny, and in particular, Manifest Destiny. He sees such premises, in all their powerful suggestiveness, shaping a national problematic of "assent." See *The Rites of Assent: Transformations in the Symbolic Construction of America* (New York: Routledge, 1993), 147-67.

[18] Jonathan Edwards, "The Millennium Probably to Dawn in America," *Works* IV, ed. C.C.Goen (New Haven: Yale Univ. Press, 1972), 355.

tribulation; his deliverance from the lions' den is indicative of his success in such matters. It is Daniel's response to his own visions that shows how "his thoughts terrified him" (Dan 4:19; cf. 7:28; 9:15; 10:7). It is precisely because of Daniel's often valiant example of daring action, that his response to his own dreams, so terror-stricken and unsure, must seem foreboding.

Such visions would daunt Americans, too. Literary critics from Harry Levin to Sacvan Bercovitch and other American cultural theorists have noted the fears within Americans as they faced such great historic prospects. It was not only a failure of will in achieving that dream (as Perry Miller has claimed), nor the necessary anxieties entailed in matching public and private identities (as Bercovitch has argued) that would cause Americans' profound distress. Nor was it even the possibility of their own kingdom's failure that most terrified these Americans. It was the very fact of an overweening narrative, moving in a comprehensive and undeviating pattern for describing their history, that was so subtly yet profoundly troubling.

When a principle of *Translatio* is spelled out into one single and singular form of self-definition, such a monolithic dream even as a program for westward settlement seemed overwhelming. It may have sounded, to some alerted ears, much the way the Elders' options did to Susanna--straitening on all sides. Seeking relief from the dark implications of the biblical Book of Daniel-- whether in sensing a sympathy with Daniel's fears, or in opting for some other version suggested within that prophetic scripture's lines--some stalwart Americans might find refuge from its implications in another Daniel story with a figure of seemingly similar outlines, but suggesting a vastly different, and humane, perspective. Such a different Daniel story appears in the apocryphal book of Susanna and the Elders.

A scripture that recalls Daniel's interpretive prowess while working against any instantiation of a single overarching version or dream, Susanna and the Elders reverberates with Susanna's own call for variant, hence viable and hopeful, statements of human potential. Susanna's voice itself rings out to remind its readers of their truly independent strengths. This would be a welcome message for early settlers precisely as they were called on to find their difficult ways toward truly better futures.[19] So, too, some centuries later, could New Americanist critics--who seek more variously genred and freely gendered versions for constructing national identity--find interest, if not comfort, in Susanna's voicings. Early or late, Americans might heed her declarations as the best source of guiding values that any scripture could supply.

Listening for Susanna in America, one first hears her most famous musical rendition in Stephen Foster's song called "Oh, Susanna!" or "Susanna,

---

[19] According to one record, a westward traveller on his way to the gold fields of California was "paddled across the Isthmus of Panama to the tune of "Oh, Susanna!" See John Spitzer, "'Oh, Susanna!': Oral Transmission and Tune Transformation," *Journal of the American Musicological Society*, XLVII (1994):91.

Don't You Cry For Me." From its first and timely appearance at the height of westward settlement, it was a huge success. Published in 1847 and picked up almost instantly by minstrel companies, it spread across the United States and overseas, "printed and reprinted" as one study of this song shows, and "arranged and rearranged by at least sixteen different publishers," including versions for voice, guitar and piano solo.[20] This song, with its funny but strangely contradictory messages, does its work for Americans in powerful and appropriate ways. While a repetitive five-tone motif comprises more than 80% of the score, these forceful repetitions are resisted by a verbal text that is crammed with disruptive juxtapositions, each of which itself is a form of oxymoron. The song's linguistic jokes are both funny and true; they speak, for example, about night time which can be included in a period that is called a day--as a result of which its rainfall too is included in the "dry weather" of the morrow:

> It rained all night the day I left,
> The weather it was dry,
> The sun so hot I froze to death,
> Susanna don't you cry...
> Oh, Susanna, don't you cry for me,
> For I come from Alabama with a banjo on my knee.

These lyrics, examined logically, show all kinds of seeming confusions that demand at least a second view. Taken for sheer delight, they further emphasize many kinds of senses--of touch (hot and cold, dry and wet), vision (day and night), emotions (laughter and tears), and even a sense of direction (from or to the north or south). Important, of course, is its own sense of music, not only of the banjo but of individual voices and sounds it mentions, including both Susanna and the banjo player. If these lyrics revel in wide possibilities, they also insist that no one version exclude--or even sing for--another, as the subtitle so famously declares. Its references to vibrant colors (a red, red rose), aromas (fresh cakes), and places (Louisiana and Alabama), in continuing verses, further draw upon a plenitude of particularized facts and feelings. All the while, that basic musical ritornello, so regular and regulative, remains within the confines of its five tones. And despite its simplicity, it presents difficulties for singing, to an amazing degree![21] The strangely conflicting sensual delights of this song would cause it to linger on in the national imagination precisely for the reason that each singer must try so valiantly to voice it. "Oh, Susanna!" virtually calls out for many discrete, even eccentric, performances, as we join

---

[20] See Spitzer, 90-91.
[21] In the recorded collections of Stephen Foster's songs that allow for lingering expressions of their highly lyrical nature, "Oh, Susanna!" is the one most often reserved for an entirely instrumental rendition. Note, for example, the Thomas Hampson CD, *American Dreamer: Songs of Stephen Foster*, Angel Recordings, 1992.

in adding, "Don't you cry for me!"

In that vein I would like to share a reading of Hawthorne's "Rappaccini's Daughter" and *The Scarlet Letter* (the novel seen as a revision six years after the earlier story), as the celebration of an unexpectedly sensuous American Susanna and her voicing. These two works offer, I believe, Hawthorne's impassioned call for his readers' own listening to a woman's voice and in doing so for giving regard to the bodily powers of a woman--such as Susanna. "Rappaccini's Daughter," Hawthorne's 1844 story emphasizes a young woman's personal and passional claims, even as a repressively theoretical onlooker struggles to get what the Preface calls "precisely the proper point of view."[22] Beatrice Rappaccini is repeatedly viewed by young Giovanni, her cautious suitor, in an enclosed Italian garden that is notable for its fountain and strange shrubs; she makes her entrances and exits through a repeatedly mentioned marble portal. The outlines of a *hortus conclusus* which are so prominent in most tellings and paintings of the Susanna story are not only visually emphasized by Hawthorne's subtle detailing of fountain, portal and enclosure, but are more broadly intertextually brought out by the many references he sprinkles throughout the story, to other enclosed gardens of mythic, artistic and literary fame.

"Rappaccini's Daughter" in its narrative content as well as in its visual details evokes elements of Susanna's story. A young woman is threatened in her enclosed garden setting by two elder figures, her father Rappaccini and his competitor Baglioni, and young Giovanni should come to saving judgment.[23] While it would seem that the elder figures in Hawthorne's story oppose one another--the father with his too-close inspection and control of his daughter, and the rival with his high-tower view as he is last seen in demonstration of his too-distant theorizing habits--Giovanni must devise a means of deflecting these two elders in order to free the woman and achieve happiness for both youthful figures. Hawthorne sets "Rappaccini's Daughter" in Padua Italy, where its actual oldest garden in Europe might remind his readers of the oldest garden in the world, or the Eden mentioned in his story--thus suggesting the great moment of such choices to be made in this garden world.

But the author underscores the story's particularly American relevance and its timely significance, less by Edenic overtones than by other means. In his preface, "From the Writings of Aubepine" Hawthorne makes reference to other examples of his works whose titles are translated into French; yet his citations repeatedly betray egregious mistakes in translation. Is he thus questioning the possibility of any correct version? Or is he playing on the very notion of

---

[22] Nathaniel Hawthorne, "Rappaccini's Daughter," in *Selected Tales and Sketches*, ed. Michael J. Colacurcio (New York: Penguin, 1987), 387.

[23] See my discussion of "Rappaccini's Daughter" as a version of *Susanna and the Elders*, "Giovanni's Garden: Hawthorne's Hope for America," *Modern Language Studies* XII (1982):75-90.

"translation" itself, in a slant reference to the failures of any single or overriding concept of *translatio*? Hawthorne's word games in this Preface include a covert but crucial reference to John O'Sullivan, his friend who is said to have coined the term "Manifest Destiny" in 1844, the same year this story was written. Could Giovanni's challenge--of finding the precise and proper point of view for understanding a woman or her fate, or his own--be an ironic condemnation of Americans' sense of their destiny as a far too singular statement of self-definition? As errors of translation in his stories' titles mount, and as the dynamics of this particular work will show, what Giovanni must learn, rather, is how to live with many possible renditions of himself and Beatrice, in an acceptance of uncertainty about love and life in all their upsetting possibilities. That would be to have "loved, not feared" this woman in the garden, as she so poignantly declares.

Carol Bensick's 1985 study of strange dark medical subtexts in Hawthorne's haunting story seems at far remove from any apocryphal American implications that I am suggesting. Yet her discoveries serve to enrich an understanding of this tale's suggestions and even of Susanna's powerful potential within it.[24] Bensick shows that Hawthorne's chosen names and settings in "Rappaccini's Daughter" replicate in amazing consistency a certain historic moment when syphilis first entered the western world: "between 1527 and 1533 in Padua." An awareness of such stark facts in Bensick's reading conjoins with my recognition of a carnal Susanna herein, since both readings emphasize a woman's--or any person's--distinctive, even palpably vulnerable, body as a basis for asserting human terms. Discrete selves proclaim disparate versions, and it is the very fact and presence of distinctive versions--including my own finding of an outspoken apocryphal Susanna in this story and Bensick's location of a disease-ridden history with verifiable features--that form our best understandings of Hawthorne, his work, and of some wider American cultural frameworks. Both Bensick's and my own readings make room for, even insist upon, the possibility of particular and personal perspectives. Doing so, both readings bring Hawthorne's readers, if not Giovanni, toward historical, and moral, and feminist--hence truly philosophical--American judgments.[25]

---

[24] Carol Marie Bensick, *La Nouvelle Beatrice: Renaissance and Romance in "Rappaccini's Daughter"* (New Brunswick: Rutgers Univ. Press, 1985),32. Bensick's subsequent essay with its revision of part of her theory is appropriate, as I will show, to an American philosophical tradition and to my reading of it as a Susanna story understood within such contexts.

[25] Bensick's more recent essay about this story finds hints of French philosophy, especially Voltaire. But her argument that this is Hawthorne's "conscious assault" mounted against a purely or merely American context for this story (77), could usefully be inverted to show this work to be Hawthorne's careful restatement of a larger concept of American philosophy. The story's moral philosophy could well be expressed by echoes of Susanna's voicings as they call for Giovanni's and the reader's attention. If Emerson's aversive thinking, as Cavell understands it, provides the very basis for an American philosophic

Notice how it is the <u>voice</u> of Beatrice that first marks Giovanni's introduction to her: it is to him "as rich as a tropical sunset...which made Giovanni, though he knew not why, think of deep hues of purple or crimson, and of perfumes heavily delectable" (391). So many senses are from the first moment at play--before any ogling begins! And when she does make her entrance, the luxuriance of her attributes contrasts with what to Giovanni seems her tensely girdled "virgin zone"; she desires to have a "perfumed breath," and Giovanni notes strange smells emanating in "oppressive exhalations" from her vicinity. She smells; she sings in "rich sweet voice." She is radiantly colorful, suggestively sexual or oppressively virginal. No wonder that Hawthorne describes Giovanni as "bewildered" and the youth himself asks, "Have I my senses?" (397).

Hawthorne is explicit in saying that "the tinge of passion" colors Beatrice's manner on her side too. An acceptance of her physicality with its discrete powers and multiple potentialities might bring this couple and this country to their senses. Lavishing attention upon the smelling, tasting, passionate sensations to be felt in this garden world as the richest means of acknowledging individual humanity, Hawthorne urges all his characters to acknowledge their own Susanna-like reactions, even as we might also do in shaping better judgments. To recognize the greatest attractions of Beatrice or Susanna would be to learn--perhaps like the townsfolk who finally share the language of Daniel's judgment--to make individual assessments as a guide for a whole community as well.

A few years after this story was published, Hawthorne's first novel appeared; in it he showed another sensuous woman standing accused of hidden sin. She faces a crowd in a town square and there are two elders in their midst. In Hawthorne's *The Scarlet Letter* of 1850, Hester Prynne is first seen facing up to the looks of Chillingworth her elder husband, and of Dimmesdale her lover who is a minister or town-elder. That these two men will soon be dwelling together in the center of this town suggests their potential for collusive accommodation. In response to one onlooker's question about this woman in one of the opening chapters, a member of the town declares, "Of truth, the Daniel who shall expound [this riddle] is yet a-wanting."[26] The book's ensuing chapters present Dimmesdale and Chillingworth as rival candidates for

---

tradition, Hawthorne's musings in that same time and place would be relevant. See Bensick, "Re-Allegorizing 'Rappaccini's Daughter'", in *New Essays on Hawthorne's Major Tales*, ed. Millicent Bell (Cambridge: Cambridge Univ. Press, 1993),74-75; and Cavell, *This New Unapproachable America: Lectures after Emerson after Wittgenstein* (Albuquerque: Living Batch Press, 1989).

[26] Nathaniel Hawthorne, *The Scarlet Letter, An Authoritative Text*, ed. Scully Bradley (New York: Norton, 2nd Ed., 1961), 49. The footnote to the quotation given in this edition cites the Book of Daniel, but more correctly, the reference here is to an apocryphal Daniel come to judgment in Susanna and the Elders, as famously cited by Shakespeare in *The Merchant of Venice* (IV,i,221).

the Daniel who can save a beset Susanna in the town's enclosed arenas. Both try to interpret signs or symptoms--whether they be upon the cope of heaven, or within a scorched heart. Yet neither can respond to Hester's story, and a tragic outcome seems inevitable when she is betrayed, not by any acts of sinful passion, but by these elders' failures to sense the desires felt by others or themselves.

Finally, however, Hester speaks out. "So said Hester Prynne," begins the last paragraph of this novel, when Hester is last seen as she "glanced her sad eyes downward at the scarlet letter." This final reference to Hester's speaking leaves her audience in the town as well as Hawthorne's own readers with the sense that she might become a prophetic figure, to save her own self. For the focus of reference in this Susanna story is reversed once again, away from staring eyes or glaring elders and away, too, from a quest for the Daniel who should come to judgment. Our final assessment of Hester is, rather, of her version-making potential, and her dawning awareness of that. She is looking at the A, not as in abstract American interpretation, but at its field, her breast and body, as her source of powerful and important voicing.[27] That is why the narrator at the start of this final paragraph reports not what Hester tells the other women, but that or "so said Hester Prynne" (emphasis added).

This woman's voicing persists, even to the very end, in the puzzling motto given as Hawthorne's last words: "On a Field, Sable, the letter A, Gules." For this last archaic term derives from tones of the throat or gullet, even as Hester's A rests upon the field of her passionate body.[28] The novel's last focus is proof of its success in transforming the harsh implications of the opening scene's iron-visaged looking at Hester to the more optimistic potential within a willing act of listening for her distinctive voice, at (or as) a better end. These words enjoin readers, too, to become party to such a promising conclusion.

A quarter-century later, in 1876, the year of the Centennial celebration of America, such an act of listening is again urged, when Henry James begins writing *The Portrait of a Lady* in response to his own declared interest in "the American" or "the Americana," as he put it, and in an authorial, national, and personal quest for further self-definitions.[29] So it is that in *The Portrait of a*

---

[27] Sharon Cameron, whose study briefly discusses this novel but focuses primarily on Hawthorne's tales, notes that Hawthorne's criticism of disembodied metaphorizations of the world appears in tales that are themselves allegorical: *The Corporeal Self: Allegories of the Body in Melville and Hawthorne* (New York: Columbia Univ. Press, 1981), Ch.2.

[28] See another discussion of Hester's downward glance and the term Gules, in Emily Miller Budick, "Sacvan Bercovitch, Stanley Cavell, and the Romance Theory of American Fiction," *PMLA* 107 (January 1992):86 ff.

[29] Adeline Tintner convincingly traces parallels between the year of the centennial, Ralph's description of Isabel as "Columbia", and James's letter to Howells in which he mentions his new novel about a female Newman, calling her an "Americana," *The Museum World of Henry James* (Ann Arbor: UMI Press, 1986), 182-3. All references given in the

Lady James calls for the voicing of a sensuous Susanna, I would argue, as his very declaration of American independence. In it, a man uncannily named Daniel wants to grant some great hand-out (or his touch) to a young woman, much the way that Rappaccini at the close of Hawthorne's story "spread[s] out his hands...in the attitude of a father imploring a blessing upon his children" (419). Words and gestures in James's novel repeatedly link such grants with the myth of Midas, or with similar instances of ideal but totalizing abstractions (Isabel from the very first finds Gardencourt "too enchanting"; she speaks of a "curse" and mentions a "golden grandfather," while Ralph on his deathbed tells her she has been "adored!"(26,65,187;479). Such comments suggest that any exceptionally empowering myths, even of an exceptionalist Daniel-given dream for America, would serve only to inhibit true vitality. Instead, Isabel--like Beatrice and like Susanna--must find her voice and make vital use of it, without relying upon the views or interpretations endowed by another, even by a Daniel. Her outspoken claim of selfhood will be her own best heritage.

Isabel makes her entrance through a portal; there she noticeably lingers. The estate she enters is a garden/court with characteristic privacy, turf, and river flowing nearby, as if to emphasize the enclosed garden quality of this story as in that of Susanna. When Isabel is asked who let her enter, she mentions "an old woman curtseying at the gate" (27), suggesting the vieille-like dame of enclosed garden stories. But what is interesting in this case is that Isabel declares the person admitted into this securely protected garden to be Isabel herself! The options then are hers: will she play the part of betrayer to herself? Or can she, in inheriting the wealth and power of Daniel, be one to interpret her own future?[30] Should she, in a variation upon the Daniel possibilities herein, become her own best judge, serving as a Daniel to her own Susanna in this garden/court rendition? Such reversals and their implications are as rife with the pitfalls as with the possibilities of the Daniel or the Susanna stories here suggested, and James seems musing on their possibilities for depicting an Americana as a woman of outspoken independence.

From the first, in further play upon hands, touching, and most probably with reverberations of the falling-into-hands dangers that Susanna speaks of in the apocryphal Susanna story itself, old Daniel Touchett speaks of his wish that someone would "feel for me" (20). (Might we also hear echoes of Foster's song about Susanna, with the negative warning, "don't you" cry or feel for me, omitted?) Such joking echoes would be further indications of this Daniel figure's inherent weakness--both as a failure of human feeling and of certain interpretive inadequacies. While Isabel just after this moment becomes the

---

text are to Henry James, *The Portrait of a Lady, An Authoritative Text*, ed. Robert D. Bamberg (New York: Norton & Co., 1975).

[30] Isabel's attempted take-over of the Daniel given powers of this novel are discussed in my essay, "Gender, Judgment, and Presumptuous Readers: The Role of Daniel in *The Portrait of a Lady*," *Henry James Review* 12(1991):218.

woman "in question," she soon enough picks up a nearby dog, and asks her own questions, as if to show how she will take matters in her own hands. She will be the one--in her words--to be "free to choose" the true version of her fate, trying to become not the betrayer but the Daniel whose judgment, perhaps quoting or simply becoming, the Susanna who can speak out, or speak for, herself.

Whatever wisdom or judgment she gains in this novel--through enduring the pain of her bad marriage, and in bearing the losses of child, friend and mentor, as in facing harsh recognitions of betrayal--becomes evident at last in the final moments Isabel is seen. When she leaves Gardencourt, she seems to be giving herself another chance, as she pauses once again at its portal. "Looking all about her she listened a little," we are told, before "putting her hand out to the door's latch" (490, emphasis added). Isabel's listening may at last indicate her awakened senses--unlike those of numbed and numbing Daniel--to "feel for" herself and others. She may now be able to act the part, not of betrayer, nor even of a biblical Daniel (they may have been the same), in imagining some singular fate for herself and others. Listening as she stands there, Isabel becomes a Susanna who trusts her senses as she stands alerted to the power of her own voicing.

In a *Portrait* so famous for devices of visual framing, fraught with controlling gazes, laced with references to paintings by Titian, Cimabue, Velasquez and others, it may seem surprising to note many instances when listening, instead, is called for. Isabel often hears music--in the Gardencourt drawing room as Madame Merle sits at the keyboard, in strange musical echoes outside Ralph's door, and later in Pansy's and her own piano playing at home. Are these the signs of James's sensual recognitions in this novel, as in Stevens' poem, and in American renditions of the Susanna story itself, as a means of better judgments to follow?

I would, accordingly, like to take note of two particular moments in *The Portrait* when still other senses become significant as part of Isabel's dawning self-realizations. F.O. Matthiessen long ago pointed out that James's revisions serve to bring out the many "aches and spirits" that intensify this novel's affective dimensions. The scenes to which I call attention would seem to subvert a sense of seeing or gazing, in favor of other kinds of sensing, in deeply felt and suggestive ways. In one rainy day encounter Madame Merle and Isabel first meet then chat while strolling, having in a previous scene begun to understand one another "so easily and quickly" (164). Sharing stories and umbrellas in this scene, they seem even to share the smells of rainy weather, as James uses terms including aroma, nostrils, inhaling, scents, wet wool, and autumnal airs in richly odorous sensations. All this, while "poor Ralph Touchett" (his full name being resonant for the lacks he, like his father, cannot but feel) is viewing them from afar: "Unable to step out of the house...[Ralph stands] at one of the windows...and, from a countenance half-rueful, half-critical," he watches Isabel and Madame Merle as they walk, and talk, and smell many things together (165). As if in extension or transformation of this scene of shared physical sensations and actually touching moments, near the end of the novel Madame Merle's daughter Pansy rests her head on Isabel's shoulder after these two younger women have been talking about Pansy's return to the convent. Isabel, we are told, "could feel her tremble" (441). Isabel, once before had "pressed her," and the term is significant in having both questioning and physical connotations. Now in their last interview, Isabel again presses Pansy, as she listens "to her, holding her breath." This moment and the phrases used to describe it once more convey both the powerful pressures of the two women's entwined listenings and other shared and sensuous or "holding" sensations. It is as if their felt stories are a matter of holding their breaths or their lives together, in a moment that is later to be remembered.

When Isabel listens, then, in the novel's final moments, it may be she has truly been called or recalled to her senses, as in those scenes with Pansy and others--and not at all, or certainly not only, in that famous last scene with Goodwood. Isabel now leaves her enclosed Gardencourt world, ready to acknowledge a plenitude of physical strains that have been aroused within her. Can she be anticipating the violet and pulsing sensations of Stevens' "Peter Quince at the Clavier"?[31] Whether or not Stevens plays out certain echoes he hears in James's work, we as readers can note the reverberations of Susanna's speaking--and her being heard, and her voicing shared--in an ongoing American tradition that still continues.

The self-conscious style of E.L.Doctorow's *The Book of Daniel* itself is the author's means of calling upon its readers' sensibilities, so as to fend off single-minded overviews. This is a story that dramatizes spying and conspiracy, wherein a sense of a some grand American idealism once again may become the worst betrayal of humanity. A brilliant post-Vietnam rendering of the McCarthy era spy trials of Julius and Ethel Rosenberg, this book's very aim seems to be that of making harsh but necessary demands upon our sensibilities, as if to gauge our own strengths.

One of the two central figures or Rosenberg sons is named Daniel; the other, representing the younger child, is a vibrant and eccentric young woman named Susan or "Susyanna."[32] She, in turn, is closely identified with the

---

[31] Two other contemporary poets, William Carlos Williams and T.S.Eliot, did write poems called "Portrait of a Lady"; however "Peter Quince" seems most truly "after"--in both following upon and responding to--certain strains of Susanna in James's *Portrait*.

[32] E.L. Doctorow, *The Book of Daniel* (New York: Signet, 1971). At a conference commemorating 40 years since the Rosenberg Trial, I asked Robert Meeropol, the younger Rosenberg son, how it felt to be translated into a feminine figure in Doctorow's novelistic rendition of his story. Meeropol's response was significant, especially in light of my sense of the power of Susanna. Ignoring the particular name of Doctorow's younger fictional child, Susan or Susyanna, Meeropol was less concerned by the gender switch than by the weakness of her figure--killed off, as he went on to add, as all forms of power or vital potential in the family itself were denied, in Doctorow's novel. But the role of Susanna in Doctorow's novel

extravagant and intensely sexual figure of her mother who represents the famous Ethel Rosenberg of the 1950s. Harsh dysfunctions and wide disjunctions within Doctorow's strange text here serve--like the discrepant versions, and strangely useful puns of the original Susanna story--to draw attention to the noticeable instabilities of minds and bodies, and the impossibilities of true knowledge in this world. Such sensations stand in stark contrast to the hero Daniel's intellectually-driven efforts to achieve some kind of sure order in formulating real and imagined personal connections. Thus a frantic quest to solve his family's history is accompanied by such bizarre efforts as the stamping of cigarette burns upon a bare behind or a last minute near-miss catch of a falling child, as if to test all kinds of contacts. This aim itself becomes dangerous, however, when a need to forge sure or certain links merely repeats or mirrors public insistence upon never-missed and unrelenting linkages, especially in a McCarthy era atmosphere. In such a world, the self-righteous forces of society will collusively and single-mindedly align themselves with invasive acts of repression, as chains of evidence straiten him, his sister, and his parents, in the direst ways that can be imagined.

When the respectable conformisms everywhere work not for but against the forces of justice, that ironic reversal in Doctorow, as in Emerson, provides the ultimate horror for American society. In Doctorow's *The Book of Daniel* as in the apocalyptic dreams of the biblical Book of Daniel, and in the conspiracies of Susanna and the Elders, monolithic dreams match up with single-minded conspiracies to become the most threatening of possibilities. If such dreams are parodied by the hero's fixation upon finding connections in this novel, they are also defied in Susyanna's sensuous madness, which is enforced by the style of this novel, even as Daniel echoes Susanna's voice in the apocryphal Daniel story, or as Doctorow offers his own *Book of Daniel* as a testimony of hers, and her mother's, truest voicing.

I close with a brief meditation on the repeated instances of punning in the literary works this survey has included--whether in the S&H Books of Redemption whose prizes are given at "Redemption centers," as Doctorow's Daniel wryly notes; or in the play upon touches, being touched, the Touchett family, and the touching moments James's Isabel learns to share; or hinted in Hester's moral wilderness, or joked about in Hawthorne's authorial references to Giovanni's im/proper point of view, or Stevens' evocation of a violet or violate evening when a "strain" is waked in the elders. All, like the puns usefully employed by Daniel at the end of Susanna and the Elders, serve to cleave apart any single version. In many ways, a double entendre reverses the

---

could be read more forcefully; while she (and her mother with whom she is closely identified) both die, they live on in the reader's horror of the contrived and collusive circumstantial evidence required by McCarthy era conformisms. It is the very reversal--as a play upon and recognition of a profound moral--of the truths implicit in Susanna's story that grants the malign elders of the 1950s only a hideous, and ironic, victory.

function of a typological framework that is based upon biblical precedents as the premise of a redemptive history. For such forceful linkage encourages a harsh conjoining of perspectives--from Isaiah or Daniel to the Puritans, to nineteenth-century dreams of westward progress, and to later theses for unlimited expansion, with still further modern presumptions of American world role. The opposite is true of word-play. To see the word and to hear it, are the pun's required separate and boldly acknowledged physical sensations. This reveling in sensation itself can widen out to affect other cultural or personal implications--questioning some terms and clarifying other problematics within other interpretive cases, as well. It could be that the very visual and aural multiplicity fundamental to the pun suggests further prospects for double and redoubled readings still unguessed--in still other narrative, temporal, corporeal or sensual interactions.

Does the ending of Susanna and the Elders then leave American readers--like Susanna unveiled at the story's center and at its central marketplace--with no cover stories for their great and national pastoral setting? Lacking some cut and dried judgment, must Americans be bathed only in everlasting conflicts and uncertainties? Like the weeping handmaidens who quaked at seeing Susanna so rudely unveiled, we should share a sense of pain in noting the brutality with which the Elders forcibly placed their hands upon Susanna's head in her moment of severest trial, as if to foist their cover-up upon her when she herself had no encompassing veil, or version, of her own to offer. But unlike those handmaidens who so promptly disappear from the scene, we do stay on to listen--somewhat like Isabel Archer, who pauses at her portal. Attending to our own vital, particular, if changing and often disturbing but surely challenging terms, and to those of others, ours is an attunement in keeping with what Cavell defines as an American philosophical tradition.[33] Joining it, we will stay tuned in for more stories of Susanna.

---

[33] Cavell uses the term "attunement," calling it an essential dynamic of a philosophy in which "human speech and community 'rest'" only on "modes of response," (*Conditions Handsome* 81-82). The title of Cavell's recent book is also relevant: *A Pitch of Philosophy* (Cambridge: Harvard Univ. Press, 1994). In one chapter he speaks of how a woman "inherits her identity" as a question of finding her voice or voicing, 136. Cavell does not, to my knowledge, mention Susanna; but he might find cause to note Americans' repeated listening to her raised voice.

Bibliography

Affanni, A. M. "Inquadramento urbanistico." In *Santa Susanna e San Bernardo alle Terme.* Rome: F.lli Palombi, 1993.

———. "Santa Susanna." In *Santa Susanna e San Bernardo alle Terme.* Rome: F.lli Palombi, 1993.

Ambrose. *De Spiritu Sancto.* 3.6.39-43.

Amours, F. J. *Scottish Alliterative Poems.* Edinburgh: Scottish Text Society, 1897.

Amussen, S. *An Ordered Society.* Oxford: Blackwell, 1988.

Anderson, G. "The Garden of Eden and Sexuality in Early Judaism." In *People of the Body: Jews and Judaism from an Embodied Perspective.* Edited by H. Eilberg-Schwartz. Albany, NY: State University of New York Press, 1992.

Apollonj Ghetti, B. *Le Chiese di Roma illustrate S. Susanna.* Rome, 1965.

Baer, Y., ed. "The Book of Josippon the Jew." In *Sefer Benzion Dinaburg.* Jerusalem: 1949.

Baker, J. H., and Milsom, S. F. C. *Sources of English Legal History.* London: Butterworth & Co., 1986.

Bakhtin, M. M. *The Dialogic Imagination: Four Essays.* Translated by C. Emerson and M. Holquist, Edited by M. Holquist. Austin, TX: University of Texas Press, 1981.

Bal, M. *Reading Rembrandt: Beyond the Word-Image Opposition.* Cambridge: Cambridge University Press, 1991.

Baris, S. D. "Giovanni's Garden: Hawthorne's Hope for America." *Modern Language Studies* XII (1982): 75-90.

———. "Gender, Judgment, and Presumptuous Readers: The Role of Daniel in *The Portrait of a Lady.*" *Henry James Review* 12(1991): 212-230.

Baumgartner, W. *Zum Alten Testament und Seiner Umwelt.* Leiden: E.J. Brill, 1959.

Bensick, C. M. *La Nouvelle Beatrice: Renaissance and Romance in "Rappaccini's Daughter".* New Brunswick, NJ: Rutgers University Press, 1985.

———. "Re-Allegorizing 'Rappaccini's Daughter'." In *New Essays on Hawthorne's Major Tales.* Edited by M. Bell, 67-82. Cambridge: Cambridge University Press, 1993.

Bercovitch, S. *The Puritan Origins of the American Self.* New Haven, CT: Yale University Press, 1975.

———. *The Rites of Assent: Transformations in the Symbolic Construction of America.* New York: Routledge, 1993.

Bezwinska, J., and Czech, D. *KL Auschwitz Seen by the SS.* New York: Howard Fertig, 1984.

Biale, R. *Women and Jewish Law.* New York: Schocken, 1984.

Bleier, R. *Science and Gender.* New York: Pergamon, 1984.

Block, K. S., ed. *Ludus Coventriae* or *The Plaie called Corpus Christi.* Oxford: Oxford University Press, 1922; 1960.

Bloom, H. *A Map of Misreading.* New York: Oxford University Press, 1975.

Bonwetsch, G.N., and Achelis, H., eds. "Exegetische und Homiletische Schriften." In *Hippolytus Werke.* Leipzig: J.C. Hinrichs, 1897.

Boyarin, D. *Carnal Israel: Reading Sex in Talmudic Culture.* Berkeley, CA: University of California Press, 1993.

Braun, M. *History and Romance in Graeco-Oriental Literature.* Oxford: Basil Blackwell, 1938.

Brock, S. P., and Harvey, S. A. *Holy Women of the Syrian Orient.* Berkeley, CA: University of California Press, 1987.

Brown, P. *The Body and Society: Men, Women and Sexual Renunciation in Early Christianity.* New York: Columbia University Press, 1988.

Brownmiller, S. *Against Our Will: Men, Women and Rape.* New York: Bantam, 1975.

Brull, N. "Das Apokryphische Susanna Buch." *Jahrbuch für judische Geschichte und Literatur* 3 (1877): 1-69.

Budick, E. M. "Sacvan Bercovitch, Stanley Cavell, and the Romance Theory of American Fiction." *PMLA* 107 (January 1992): 78-91.

Burrus, V. "Word and Flesh: The Bodies and Sexuality of Ascetic Women in Christian Antiquity." *Journal of Feminist Studies in Religion* 10 (1994): 27-52.

Cabrol, F., and Leclercq, H. *Dictionnaire d'Archéologie Chrétienne et de Liturgie.* Vol. XV, Paris: Letouzey et Ane, 1953.

Cameron, S. *The Corporeal Self: Allegories of the Body in Melville and Hawthorne.* New York: Columbia University Press, 1981.

Cave, T. *Recognitions: A Study in Poetics.* Cambridge, England: Clarendon, 1988.

Cavell, S. *This New Unapproachable America: Lectures after Emerson after Wittgenstein.* Albuquerque, NM: Living Batch Press, 1989.

———. *Conditions Handsome and Unhandsome: The Constitution of Emersonian Perfectionism.* Chicago: University of Chicago Press, 1990.

———. *A Pitch of Philosophy.* Cambridge, MA: Harvard University Press, 1994.

Caws, M. A. *The Art of Interference: Stressed Readings in Verbal & Visual Texts.* Princeton, NJ: Princeton University Press, 1989.

Chadwick, H. *The Early Church.* Harmondsworth: Penguin, 1967.

Charles, R. H. *The Apocrypha and Pseudepigrapha of the Old Testament.* 2 vols. Oxford: Clarendon Press, 1913.

Cohen, Y. "Ma'se shoshanna." In *Encyclopedia of Narrative Themes in the Literature of the Jewish People*, Edited by Y. Elstein. in preparation.

Cooper, S. "Newgate: An Old-New Town in the Negev." Ph.D. diss., Catholic University of America, 1978.

Delange, N. *Apocrypha: Jewish Literature of the Hellenistic Age.* New York: Viking, 1978.

Delehaye, H. *The Legends of the Saints.* Notre Dame, IN: University of Notre Dame Press, 1962.

Dennis, P. A. "The Role of the Drunk in an Oaxacan Village." *American Anthropologist* 77 (1975).

Doctorow, E. L. *The Book of Daniel.* New York: Signet, 1971.

Doran, R. "The Additions to Daniel." *Harpers Bible Commentary.* San Francisco: Harper and Row, 1988.

Doyle, A. I. "The Shaping of the Vernon and Simeon Manuscripts." In *Chaucer and Middle English Studies in Honor of Rossell Hope Robbins.* Edited by B. Rowland. Kent: Kent State University Press, 1974.

Edwards, J. "The Millennium Probably to Dawn in America." In *Works* IV, Edited by C.C. Goen. New Haven, CT: Yale University Press, 1972.

Emerson, R. W. *Selections from Ralph Waldo Emerson.* Edited by S.E. Whicher. Boston: Houghton Mifflin, 1957.

Epstein, I., ed. *The Babylonian Talmud.* London: The Soncino Press, 1938.

Eusebius, *Ecclesiastical History.* Book 6, Loeb Classical Library. Vol II, J.E.L. Oulton, trans. Cambridge, MA: Harvard University Press 1932), pp. 29-31.

Fisch, H. *Poetry With A Purpose: Biblical Poetics and Interpretation.* Bloomington, IN: Indiana University Press, 1988.

———. "Power and Constraint: Covenantal Hermeneutics in Milton." In *Summoning: Ideas of the Covenant and Interpretive Theory*. Edited by E. Spolsky, 1-24. Albany, NY: State University of New York Press, 1993.

Flusser, D. "The Author of Sefer Yosippon, His Character and Period." *Zion* 18 (1953): 109-126.

———, ed. *The Josippon*. 2 vols. Jerusalem: Mosad Bialik, 1978-80.

Forshall, J., and Madden, F., eds. *The Wycliffite Bible*. 4 vols. Oxford: Oxford University Press, 1850.

Foster, S. *American Dreamer: Songs of Stephen Foster*, Angel Recordings, 1992. Thomas Hampson Compact Disc.

Fried, M. *Absorption and Theatricality: Painting & Beholder in the Age of Diderot*. Berkeley, CA: University of California Press, 1980.

Funk, R. W. *Language, Hermeneutic and the Word of God*. New York: Harper and Row, 1968.

Garrard, M. D. "Artemisia and Susanna." In *Feminism and Art History: Questioning the Litany*, Edited by N. Braude and M. D. Garrard. New York: Harper and Row, 1982.

Garter, T. *The Most Virtuous and Godly Susanna* (1578), Malone Society Reprints, Oxford: Oxford University Press, 1937.

Gaster, M., ed. and trans., *The Chronicles of Jerahmeel*. Oriental Translation Fund, Vol. 4, 1899.

Geiger, L. *Johannes Reuchlin*. Leipzig, 1870.

The Geneva Bible. A facsimile of the 1560 edition. Madison, WI: University of Wisconsin Press, 1969.

Ginzberg, L. *The Legends of the Jews*. Philadelphia: Jewish Publication Society, 1967.

Goodman, C. *How Superior Powers Oght to be Obeyd*. Facsimile Text Society, New York: Columbia University Press, 1931.

Gosynhill, E. *Mulierum Paean*. London, 1542.

Greenblatt, S. *Shakespearean Negotiations: The Circulation of Social Energy in Reniassance England*. Berkeley, CA: University of California Press, 1988.

Grelot, P. "Les Versions Grecques de Daniel." *Biblica* 47 (1966): 381-402.

Gross, K. *Spenserian Poetics: Idolatry, Iconoclasm, and Magic*. Ithaca: Cornell University Press, 1985.

Haigh, C. *Elizabeth I*. London: Longman, 1988.

Hartman, L. and Di Lella, A. A. "The Book of Daniel." *Anchor Bible 23*. Garden City, NY: Doubleday, 1978.

Hastings, J., ed. *Dictionary of the Bible*. 4 vols. London and New York: T.T. Clark, 1902.

Hawthorne, N. *The Scarlet Letter, An Authoritative Text*. 2d ed., Edited by S. Bradley. New York: Norton, 1961.

———. "Rappaccini's Daughter." In *Selected Tales and Sketches*. Edited by M. J. Colacurcio. New York: Penguin, 1987.

Henderson, K., and McManus, B. *Half Humankind*. Urbana, IL: University of Illinois Press, 1985.

Hertling, L., and Kirschbaum, E. *The Roman Catacombs and Their Martyrs*. Milwaukee, Bruce Publishing Co., 1956.

Hippolytus, "Fragments from his Commentaries." S.D.F. Salmond, trans. Vol VI, *Ante-Nicene Christian Library*. Vol. X. Edinburgh: T.& T. Clark 1869.

———. *Commentaire sur Daniel*. Edited by M. Lefèvre. Paris, 1947.

Horner, S. "Spiritual Truth and Sexual Violence: the Old English Juliana, Anglo-Saxon Nuns, and the Discourse of Female Monastic Enclosure." *Signs* 19 (1994): 658-675.

Hudson, A. "John Purvey: A Reconsideration of the Evidence for his Life and Writings." *Viator* 12 (1981): 355-80.

——, ed. *English Wycliffite Sermons.* 4 vols. Oxford: Oxford University Press, 1987-1995.

——, ed. "The Testimony of William Thorpe." In *Two Wycliffite Texts.* Oxford: Oxford University Press, 1993.

Hughes, H. M. *The Ethics of Jewish Apocryphal Literature.* London: Robert Culley, 1910.

James, H. *The Portrait of a Lady, An Authoritative Text,* Edited by R. D. Bamberg. New York: Norton & Co., 1975.

Janeway, E. *Powers of the Weak.* New York: Morrow Quill, 1981.

Jeffrey, D. L. "Chaucer and Wyclif: Biblical Hermeneutic and Literary Theory in the XIVth Century." In *Chaucer and Scriptural Tradition.* Ottawa: University of Ottawa Press, 1984.

——. *The Law of Love: English Spirituality in the Age of Wyclif.* Grand Rapids, MI: Eerdmans, 1988.

Jellinek, A. ed., *Beth-Hamidrash.* Vol 6, 2nd ed. Jerusalem: Bamberger and Wahrmann, 1938.

Jerome, *Commentariorum in Danielem Libri III (IV).* Edited by F. Glorie. S. Hieronymi Presbyteri Opera, Pars 1, Opera Exegetica 5. Corpus Christianorum Series Latina 75A. Brepols: Turnholt, 1964.

Jonson, B. *The Alchemist.* In *Ben Jonson.* Vol. 5, Edited by C.H. Herford and P. Simpson. Oxford: Clarendon, 1937.

Jordan, C. "Woman's Rule in Sixteenth-Century British Political Thought." *Renaissance Quarterly* XI(1987): 421-51.

Jordan, M. *Ordering Wisdom: The Hierarchy of Philosophical Discourses in Aquinas.* Notre Dame, IN: University of Notre Dame Press, 1986.

Jungmann, J. A. *The Early Liturgy to the Time of Gregory the Great.* Notre Dame, IN: University of Notre Dame Press, 1959.

Kellogg, A. L. "Susannah and the Merchant's Tale." *Speculum* 35 (1960): 275-279.

Kennedy, V. L. *The Saints of the Canon of the Mass.* 2nd ed. Vatican City: Pontificio Istituto di Archeologia Cristiana, 1963.

Kirschbaum, E., ed. *Lexicon der Christlichen Ikonographie.* Rome-Freiburg-Basel-Vienna: Herder, 1968.

Knox, J. *The First Blast of the Trumpet Against the Monstrous Regiment of Women.* Facsimile of 1558 edition, Amsterdam: Theatarum Orbis Terrarum, Ltd., 1972.

Kolodny, A. "Letting Go Our Grand Obsessions: Notes Toward a New Literary History of the American Frontiers." *American Literature* 64 (1991): 1-18.

Krautheimer, R. *Corpus Basilicarum Christianorum Romae.* Vatican City: Pontificio Istituto di Archeologia Cristiana, 1937.

Lacks, R. *Women and Judaism: Myth, History and Struggle.* New York: Doubleday, 1980.

LaCocque, A. *The Feminine Unconventional, Four Subversive Figures in Israel's Tradition.* Minneapolis: Fortress, 1990.

Leach, M. C. "Ruben's *Susanna and the Elders* in Munich and Some Early Copies." *Print Review* 5 (1976): 120-27.

Lerner, G. *The Creation of Patriarchy.* Oxford: Oxford University Press, 1986.

Levi, I. "L'Histoire de 'Suzanne et les deux Vieillards' dans la Littérature Juive." *Revue des Etudes Juives* 95 (1933): 157-71.

Levin, C. "Queens and Claimants: Political Insecurity in Sixteenth-Century England." In *Gender, Ideology, and Action: Historical Perspectives on Women's Public Lives.* Edited by J. Sharistanian. New York: Greenwood Press, 1986.

Levine, A. J. "'Hemmed In On Every Side:' Jews and Women in the Book of Susanna." In *Reading From This Place*. Edited by S. Segovia and M. Tolbert. Philadelphia: Fortress Press, 1994.

Levi-Strauss, C. *Totemism*. Boston: Beacon, 1963.

Lifton, R. J. *The Nazi Doctors*. New York: Basic Books, 1986.

Lightfoot, J. *Commentary on the New Testament from the Talmud and Hebraica*. 4 vols. Oxford: Oxford University Press, 1859. Reprint. Gloucester, MA: Hendrickson, 1989.

Littlewood, A. R. "Romantic Paradises: The Role of the Garden in the Byzantine Romance." *Byzantine and Modern Greek Studies* 5 (1979): 95-114.

MacDonald, S. "Theory of Knowledge." In *The Cambridge Companion to Aquinas*. Edited by N. Kretzmann and E. Stump. Cambridge: Cambridge University Press, 1993.

——., and Stump, E., eds. "Wisdom: Will, Belief, and Moral Goodness." In *Aquinas's Moral Theory*. Ithaca, NY: Cornell University Press, forthcoming.

Maclear, J. F. "New England and the Fifth Monarchy: The Quest for Millennium in Early American Puritanism." *William and Mary Quarterly* 32 (1975): 223-60.

Magnus, A. *Commentarius in librum Danielis prophetae*. Opera Omnia 8. Lyons: Aschendorff, 1651.

Marks, H. "Pauline Theology and Revisionary Criticism." *Journal of the American Academy of Religion* 52 (1984): 71-92.

Matthew, F. D., ed. *The English Works of Wyclif*. London: Kegan Paul, Trench and Trubner, 1880, 1902.

May, H. G., and Metzger, B. M., eds. *The Oxford Annotated Bible with the Apocrypha*. New York: Oxford University Press, 1965.

Mazzarino, S. *L'impero Romano*. Vol. II. Rome-Bari: Laterza, 1973.

Metzger, B. M. *An Introduction to the Apocrypha*. New York: Oxford University Press, 1957.

——., and Murphy, R. E. *The New Oxford Annotated Bible With the Apocryphal/Deuterocanonical Books*. New York: Oxford University Press, 1991.

Meyer, K., and Baris, S. D. "Reading the Score of 'Peter Quince at the Clavier': Stevens, Music, and the Visual Arts." *Wallace Stevens Journal* 12 (1988): 56-67.

Michel, E. *Die Mosaiken von S. Costanza in Rom*. Leipzig, 1912.

Midrash Aggada II. Vayikra.

Miskimin, A., ed. *Susannah: An Alliterative Poem of the Fourteenth Century*. New Haven-London: Yale University Press, 1969.

Missale Romanum ex Decreto Sacrosancti. 13th ed. Concilii Tridentini restitutum. S. Pii V Pontificis Maximi jussu editum. Turin-Rome, 1961.

Moore, C. A., ed. *Daniel, Esther, and Jeremiah: The Additions*. Anchor Bible 44. Garden City, NJ: Doubleday, 1977.

Mozley, J. H. "Susanna and the Elders: Three Medieval Poems." *Studi Medievali*, n.s. 3 (1930): 27-52.

Narkiss, B. "The Bible: Translations - Greek." *Encyclopedia Judaica*. Jerusalem: Keter Publishing House, 1972.

Neale, J. E. *Queen Elizabeth*. New York: Harcourt, Brace and Co., 1934.

Neuman, A. "Josippon and the Apocrypha." *JQR* 43 (1952-53): 1-26.

Newman, B. *Sister of Wisdom: St. Hildegard's Theology of the Feminine*. Berkeley, CA: University of California Press, 1987.

Origen, *The Writings of Origen*. Vol. I. Edited by A. Roberts and J. Donaldson. eds. *Ante-Nicene Christian Library*. Vol. X. Edinburgh: T.& T. Clark 1869.

Pervo, R. I. "Aseneth and Her Sisters: Women in Jewish Narrative and in the Greek Novels." In *"Women Like This": New Perspectives on Jewish Women in the Greco-Roman World.* Edited by A. J. Levine. Atlanta, GA: Scholars Press, 1991.

Plantinga, A. *Warrant and Proper Function.* Oxford: Oxford University Press, 1993.

Radin, P. *The Trickster: A Study in American Indian Mythology.* New York: Schocken, 1972.

Reardon, B. P. *The Form of Greek Romance.* Princeton, NJ: Princeton University Press, 1991.

Reuchlin, J. *Der Augenspiegel,* fol. 32b.

Riga, P. "Historia Susanne." In *Aurora: Petri Rigae Biblia Versificata.* Edited by C.S.C Beichner. 2 vols. Notre Dame, IN: Notre Dame University Press, 1965.

Roston, M. *Biblical Drama in England.* London: Faber and Faber, 1968.

Samaha, J. "Gleanings from Local Criminal-Court Records: Sedition amongst the 'Inarticulate' in Elizabethan Essex." *Journal of Social History* 8(1975): 61-79.

Sayers, D. *Omnibus of Crime.* London, 1929.

Scalingi, P. "The Scepter or the Distaff: The Question of Female Sovereignty, 1516-1607." *Historian* 41(1978): 59-75.

Sereny, G. *Into That Darkness: An Examination of Conscience.* New York: Vintage, 1983.

Sexton, J. *The Slandered Woman in Shakespeare,* English Literary Studies, no. 12, Victoria, British Columbia.: University of Victoria Press, 1978.

Shakespeare, W. *Measure for Measure.* Edited by J.W. Lever. Arden edition. London: Methuen, 1965, 1984.

Sharpe. J. A. *Defamation and Sexual Slander in Early Modern England,* Borthwick Papers, no. 58, Borthwick Institute of Historical Research, University of York, 1980.

Shepard, T. *God's Great Plot: The Paradoxes of Puritan Piety,* Edited by M. McGiffert. Amherst, MA: University of Massachusetts Press, 1972.

Simon, M., trans. "Midrash Rabbah: Song of Songs." In *The Midrash.* Vol. IX. London: Soncino Press, 1939.

Sollerio, J. B., Pinio, J., Cupero, G., and Boschio, P., eds. *Acta Sanctorum.* Edited by J. Carnandet "Augusti Tomus Secundus." Paris-Rome: V. Palme, 1867.

Spitzer, J. "'Oh, Susanna!': Oral Transmission and Tune Transformation." *Journal of the American Musicological Society* XLVII (1994): 90-136.

Srawley, J. H. *The Early History of the Liturgy.* 2d ed. London: Cambridge University Press, 1947.

Stallybrass, P. "Transvestism and the 'Body Beneath': Speculating on the Boy Actor." In *Erotic Politics.* Edited by S. Zimmerman. London: Routledge, 1992.

Statutes of the Realm. London, 1587.

Stegman, M. O. "Wallace Stevens and Music: A Discography of Stevens' Record Collection." *Wallace Stevens Journal* 3 (1979): 79-97.

Steinberg, L. "Picasso's Sleepwatchers." In *Other Criteria: Confrontations with Twentieth Century Art.* New York: Oxford University Press, 1972.

Steiner, W. *Pictures of Romance: Form Against Context in Painting and Literature.* Chicago: Chicago University Press, 1988.

Stevens, W. "Peter Quince at the Clavier." In *Collected Poems of Wallace Stevens.* New York: Knopf, 1954.

Stump, E. "Aquinas on the Foundations of Knowledge." *Canadian Journal of Philosophy* suppl. vol. 17 (1991): 125-158.

Tanhuma. Vayikra 10.

Tintner, A. *The Museum World of Henry James.* Ann Arbor, MI: University of Michigan Press, 1986.

Todd, J. H., ed. *An Apology for Lollard Doctrine*. London: Camden Society, 1842.

Tov, E. *Textual Criticism of the Hebrew Bible*. Philadelphia: Fortress Press, 1992.

Trible, P. *Texts of Terror*. Philadelphia: Fortress Press, 1984.

Turner, V. *Dramas, Fields, and Metaphors: Symbolic Action in Human Society*. Ithaca, NY: Cornell University Press, 1974.

Vodret, R. "La decorazione interna." In *Santa Susanna e San Bernardo alle Terme*. Rome: F.lli Palombi, 1993.

Von Hutten, U. *Letters of Obscure Men*. Heidelberg: Weissbach, 1924.

Walker, S. C. *Seven Ways of Looking at Susanna*. Provo, UT: University of Utah Press, 1984.

Watt, T. *Cheap Print and Popular Piety, 1550-1640*. Cambridge: Cambridge University Press, 1991.

Welter, B. "The Feminization of American Religion, 1800-1860." In *Clio's Consciousness Raised: New Perspectives on the History of Women*. Edited by M. Hartman and L. Banner. New York: Harper and Row, 1974.

Williams, R. "The Bloudy Tenet of Persecution." in *The Puritans*, Vol I, Edited by P. Miller and Thomas Johnson. New York: Harper & Row, 1938, 1963.

Wilpert, J. *Roma Sotterranea: Le Pitture delle Catacombe Romane*. Rome: Lefebvre and Co., 1903.

———. *I Sarcofagi Cristiani Antichi*. Rome: Pontificio Istituto di Archeologia Cristiana, 1929.

Witte, J., Jr. "The Transformation of Marriage Law in the Lutheran Reformation." In *The Weightier Matters of the Law: Essays on Law and Religion*. Atlanta, GA: Scholars Press, 1988.

Ziegler, J. ed., *Susanna, Daniel, Bel et Draco, Septuaginta: Vestus Testamentum Graecum*. Gottingen: Vandenhoeck and Ruprecht, 1954.

Zimmerman, F. "The Story of Susanna and Its Original Language." *JQR* 48 (1957): 236-41.